JOURNEY
TO THE
WILDERNESS

JOURNEY
to the
WILDERNESS

*War, Memory, and a Southern
Family's Civil War Letters*

Frye Gaillard
Foreword by Steven Trout

NewSouth Books
Montgomery

NewSouth Books
105 S. Court Street
Montgomery, AL 36104

Copyright © 2015 by Frye Gaillard. Foreword © 2015 by Steven Trout.
All rights reserved under International and Pan-American Copyright
Conventions. Published in the United States by NewSouth Books, a division of
NewSouth, Inc., Montgomery, Alabama.

The map illustration on pages 26–27 is by Linda Aldridge. The map on page 8
was provided by the Doy Leale McCall Rare Book and Manuscript Library at the
University of South Alabama. All other photographs and illustrations are
from the author's family archives.

Publisher's Cataloging-in-Publication data

Gaillard, Frye, 1946–
Journey to the wilderness: war, memory, and a southern family's Civil War letters /
Frye Gaillard ; foreword by Steven Trout
p. cm.
Includes index.

ISBN 978-1-58838-312-9 (hardcover)
ISBN 978-1-60306-361-6 (ebook)

1. United States—History—Civil War, 1861-1865—Personal narratives,
Confederate. I. Title.

2014957409

Design by Randall Williams

Printed in the United States of America
by Bang Printing

To the family of Colonel Fred E. Gaillard
for preserving the letters of Franklin Gaillard,
our eloquent ancestor in common;

and to my aunt, Mary Gaillard,
and my grandfather, S. P. Gaillard,
who taught me that history is a living thing

CONTENTS

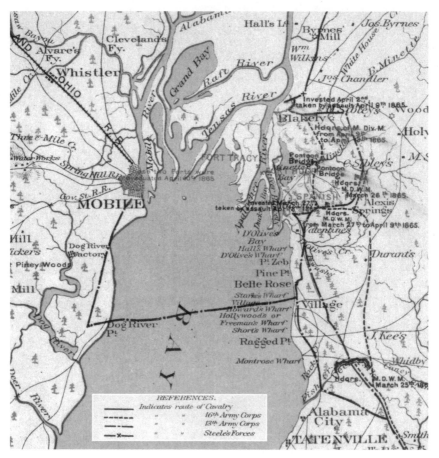

Detail of Union map of troop movements of March–April 1865 in southern Alabama. Fort Blakely is across from Mobile at the upper end of Mobile Bay. (Today's familiar towns of Daphne and Fairhope on the Eastern Shore of Mobile Bay did not yet exist.) The map, credited to Lt. S. E. McGregory, U.S. Army of West Mississippi, was provided through the courtesy of the Doy Leale McCall Rare Book and Manuscript Library at the University of South Alabama.

FOREWORD

A JOURNEY TO THE WILDERNESS . . . AND TO FORT BLAKELY

STEVEN TROUT

Some years ago, the History Channel offered a disturbing glimpse of what it must *really* have been like to fight in the American Civil War: as part of a documentary on the battle of Antietam, a team of artillery enthusiasts set up rows of oil drums, filled them with water mixed with red food coloring, and then fired at them with actual cannons from the 1860s. The results were, to put it mildly, dramatic. Travelling at over a thousand miles per hour, twelve-pound cannon balls ripped some of the containers in half, sent others tumbling end over end, and splattered scarlet liquid twenty feet or more into the air. And bear in mind that these were metal drums, not fragile vessels made of flesh.

Realizing what artillery projectiles could do—to say nothing of small-arms ammunition like the ubiquitous minie ball, which flattened upon impact, shattering bones in the process—was just one facet of what Civil War soldiers meant when they referred to the experience of combat as "seeing the elephant." The sights and sounds of battle were so overwhelming and hallucinatory, so incomprehensibly at odds with ordinary experience, that only a circus metaphor would do. You had either seen the elephant or you hadn't. There was no use in describing.

So, after the war, most veterans didn't try. On both sides of the Mason-Dixon Line, a kind of Victorian grand eloquence, far removed from the terror and brutality of combat, became the signature language of the war's memory. Organizations like the United Daughters of the Confederacy, which played a leading role in Southern war commemoration, celebrated the conflict as a time of "honor" and "gallantry," a word that still floated in the humid air of Mobile, Alabama, nearly a century later, forming part of Frye Gaillard's childhood. Thousands of books on the Civil War appeared before 1900. But only a few, such as Horace Porter's surprisingly graphic *Campaigning with Grant* or Stephen Crane's *The Red Badge of Courage* (written, ironically enough, by a non-veteran born in 1871), come close to preparing a present-day reader for that gruesome oil-drum demonstration.

The ground where the Blue and the Gray once clashed likewise gives little indication of the war's terrible realities. In the late 1800s—as white Northerners and Southerners settled into a comfortable state of reconciliation, tacitly agreeing to the continued subjugation of black Americans—the five Civil War sites of Antietam, Chickamauga-Chattanooga, Gettysburg, Shiloh, and Vicksburg became the nation's first official battlefield parks. Dotted with stirring memorials and markers, these places of remembrance (or is it forgetting?) remain among the loveliest spots in the United States, manicured green spaces whose beauty and peacefulness belie the violence that inspired their preservation.

And when legions of so-called reenactors periodically gather on these hallowed grounds, the resulting spectacle hides more of the true face of war than it reveals, a fact for which both the reenactors and their audience should be grateful. The clouds of black-powder smoke and the thunderous discharge of weapons are presumably realistic enough. But the playacting leaves out the very things that make war *war*—the bowel-loosening fear, the rage, the confusion, and, of course, the blood. Reenacting may have its virtues, but it hardly offers a glimpse of the elephant.

In his thoughtful presentation of the family letters in this volume, Frye Gaillard reminds us that the Civil War, like all wars, was brutal and ugly. In his own way, he points a cannon at some oil drums. Readers quickly realize that the book's title—*Journey to the Wilderness*—holds a double meaning. Arranged chronologically, the letters carry us from the opening of the rebellion, which most (but not all) of Frye's Southern ancestors welcomed, to the terrible Battle of the Wilderness in 1864, where the Gaillard family's most zealous Confederate met his end. But the book also journeys backwards in time, as Frye peels away layers of cultural myth and family legend to expose long-hidden pain, ambivalence, and horror. This foreword briefly considers what a journey to the Wilderness means in terms of military history—or, stated more baldly, the history of organized killing. And then it will turn to a more obscure corner of the conflict, one that nevertheless had an important place in the Gaillard family's wartime experience.

OF COURSE, AMERICANS DON'T like to dwell on the violence and brutality of the Civil War—strangely, our most beloved war—and have assiduously avoided doing so for much of the past 150 years. We prefer romance and reenactments. As Frye makes clear, in the mid-twentieth-century Alabama of his youth one could not speak of the events of 1861 to 1865 without kneeling before the conviction that the Confederacy lost the war, yes, but lost it *gloriously*. Within this framework of consolatory myth, known as the Lost Cause, ordinary rebel soldiers fought with superhuman endurance and resolve—certainly never running from the enemy!—and were led by commanders who epitomized strategic brilliance and, of course, gallantry. By the 1950s, Lee, Jackson, Stuart, Mosby, and Forrest—the vaunted pantheon of Confederate generalship—had all acquired cult followings, which to some extent they still enjoy today, as heroic underdogs who consistently outmaneuvered their adversaries, but whose valiant efforts were doomed by Yankee industrialism and superior numbers.

Cast in the romantic terms of the Lost Cause, the rebellion assumed a reckless grandeur. But missing from the picture was the very thing that gave this body of myth its urgency—namely, the utter, annihilating destruction that the conflict visited upon the Confederacy. Indeed, for the American South, the war was by any measure an unmitigated disaster. Nearly one in four Confederate soldiers—an estimated 300,000—died either from combat or disease, a catastrophe that left its mark, in one way or another, on nearly every household in the Confederate states. But the loss of so many young men was only part of it. By the time of Lee's surrender at Appomattox, the region's central railroads had been destroyed, their rails creatively corkscrewed around trees and telegraph poles; its population reduced to a state of semi-starvation; and its major cities left in smoldering ruin. Photographs of Richmond, Atlanta, or Charleston in 1865 look shockingly like images of Dresden, Berlin, or Hiroshima in 1945.

The similarity is hardly coincidental. Many historians contend that the War Between the States represents one of the world's earliest manifestations of so-called total war—war, that is, waged by entire populations, underwritten by entire economies, and pursued with the objective of victory at any price through any means necessary, including the targeting of enemy civilians. Chivalry and dash, of the sort traditionally attributed to the Confederacy's larger-than-life battle commanders, perhaps had a small place in the drama of 1861 to 1865, but the relentless demands of this new total war essentially defined the conflict. In their all-out bid to win, the Union and Confederate governments both implemented conscription. Both ruthlessly suppressed dissent and curtailed civil rights (as regimes in the midst of total war have done ever since). Both neglected enemy prisoners of war, thereby anticipating twentieth-century war crimes. And once military manpower began to run in short supply, both mobilized black soldiers. Thanks to the extraordinary film *Glory*, the achievements of African American troops in the Union Army are well known. But it is often forgotten that by March 1865, one month before the fall of Richmond, the Confederate Army's need for fresh bodies to fill its tattered ranks became so urgent that Jefferson Davis approved the enlistment of slaves. Needless to say, this measure directly contradicted the longstanding Southern argument that blacks were, by nature, infantile and therefore in need of the structure and security supposedly offered by the slave system. As the Confederacy discovered, the inexorable logic of total war has a way of drastically altering the aims and values of societies swept up in it.

As one of the world's earliest examples of this new mode of mass violence, the American Civil War also offered a lesson that European observers would have done well to recognize: provided that the adversaries are equally committed, war fought in this way and on this kind of scale cannot be resolved quickly or with minimal loss of life or property. When the Allies and Central Powers mobilized their armies in August 1914, they did so with the expectation of swift victory. Nearly every belligerent nation imagined seizing the capital city of its chief adversary after just a few weeks of fighting. But it was not to be. What came to be known as the Great War—and, after that, as the First *World* War—soon degenerated into a contest of grinding attrition, of prolonged trench warfare, which should have surprised no one. A similar thing had happened in America's Great War half a century earlier.

In both conflicts, the gap between tactics and technology produced unforeseen carnage and pushed soldiers into what the literary critic Paul Fussell aptly called the "troglodyte world" of the trenches. In the First World War, as is well known, the modern machine gun (invented by an American, Hiram Maxim, in 1884) suddenly gave a handful of men the ability to mow down hundreds. As a result, soldiers had no choice but to dig in, and whenever they tried to storm enemy trench-lines manned by machine-gunners, the results were less battles than massacres: in the 1916 Battle of the Somme, nearly 60,000 British troops were killed or wounded on the first day, many struck down just moments after entering no-man's land. It would take four years—and millions of casualties—before tacticians on both sides developed methods of successfully overcoming the trench deadlock.

Military doctrine and weaponry were likewise out of sync in 1861. At the start of the American Civil War, the Union and Confederate armies essentially followed Napoleonic-era tactics, which called for tightly packed rows of men trained in the art of delivering rapid-fire volleys at similarly congested formations of enemy soldiers. In the early nineteenth century, this approach to black-powder warfare made sense: the smooth-bore muskets of that era were notoriously inaccurate, hence the need to fire them in masse. But by 1861, the rifled minie ball had arrived. Even when discharged by a weapon in the trembling hands of a soldier half-blind from fear (a probably accurate description of most men in the midst of a Civil War battle), rifled projectiles stood a better chance of hitting their targets. And hit them they did. Antiquated tactics plus the minie ball equaled injury and death on a then-unprecedented scale, as seen in the shocking numbers of dead and wounded for major battles in 1862 and 1863. Casualties (Union and Confederate combined) at Shiloh: roughly 23,000; Antietam: 22,000 (all in one day); Gettysburg: 50,000; Chickamauga: 30,000. Designed to pass through the human frame "like butter" (according to one of the experts on that Antietam documentary), artillery projectiles contributed their share of terror to these battles, but historians estimate that the innocuous-looking minie ball did most of the maiming and killing.

However, the bloodiest phase of the American Civil War, even worse than the campaigns of 1862 and 1863, occurred when this Napoleonic style of battle, made ever more costly by improved firepower, mutated into something much closer to the ghastly attrition warfare of the 1914–18 Western Front. In the summer of 1864, the Union Army of the Potomac, by then under the command of Ulysses S. Grant, pushed southward toward the Confederate capital of Richmond and clashed with Lee's celebrated Army of Northern Virginia in a series of dreadful battles whose combined casualties numbered more than 100,000. Grant's plan of attack in what came to be known as the Overland Campaign was simple. His experience at Shiloh in 1862, where more soldiers died than in *all* of America's previous wars combined, had convinced him that there would be no easy way out, that victory would require nothing less than the total defeat of the Confederate military through a series of necessarily bloody and protracted operations. In the western theater, where Grant rose to fame, this prognosis set him apart as a true fighting general and won him Lincoln's admiration and support. Now, moving over land that had seen armies come and go since the earliest days of the war, he would press Lee's forces until they cracked. A new and terrible spirit seemed to take hold of the conflict, a spirit more removed than ever from romance or gallantry.

As the Union army inched toward Richmond, and battle followed upon battle, it became unclear at times which side would collapse first, even though Grant held a nearly two-to-one advantage over his opponent. The campaign turned into a meat-grinder for both armies. At the Wilderness, where Franklin Gaillard's luck finally ran out, Lee pursued his usual strategy of defense through attack—if the word "strategy" can be applied to the wild melee that resulted when the two armies collided amid a tract of jungle-like foliage. But at the notorious battle of Cold Harbor, a month later, the Confederate commander did something uncharacteristic: he ordered his troops to construct defensive earthworks and to let the federals come to them. The result was one of the most lopsided battles of the entire war, an American version, if you will, of the first day of the Somme. Lee's army suffered approximately 1,500 casualties at Cold Harbor, but thanks to a series of disastrous frontal assaults, estimates of Union losses run as high as 7,000.

And as if the Overland Campaign did not already contain enough ominous portents of twentieth-century warfare, its final phase, Grant's protracted siege of the Confederate capital and the neighboring city of Petersburg (a rail hub vital to Richmond's defense) anticipated the conditions of World War I trench warfare with eerie exactitude. From midsummer 1864 until the spring of 1865, the two armies occupied parallel systems of trenches and fortifications that extended for more than 40 miles. Like later combatants on the European Western Front, soldiers snatched what sleep they could during the day. Nighttime meant more piling up of dirt and sandbags. Sharpshooters (what we would today call "snipers") patiently scanned the trench lines, picking off anyone who dared to appear in the open. At the same time, in an ironic twist, the Overland Campaign moved underground, as engineers tunneled beneath enemy positions and laid explosives. Indeed, it was here—in this final mega-siege—that the notorious Battle of the Crater occurred on July

30, 1864. After detonating a mine so massive that it instantaneously atomized several square acres of earthworks (together with an entire Confederate regiment), Union troops foolishly rushed into the gigantic bowl left behind from the explosion. Confederate survivors of the blast gathered on the crater's lip and slaughtered them.

Given such grotesquery, it is perhaps little wonder that despite its scale and historical importance the Overland Campaign has never loomed particularly large in collective memory of the Civil War. What people remember is what came next: Lee's inevitable abandonment of Richmond (once the rail lines leading into the city were lost), and his desperate retreat west to Appomattox, where, hemmed in and hopelessly outnumbered, he surrendered to Grant on April 9, 1865. The modern-day congestion in northern Virginia also hampers memory of what happened there in the summer of 1864. Retail corridors and housing developments, all part of the greater Washington, D.C., megalopolis, now cover much of the territory where the bloodiest campaign of the Civil War occurred. Traffic noise penetrates into all but the deepest recesses of the Wilderness—or, rather, the section of that once primeval forest that remains.

BUT THERE IS ONE place in the United States where one can still see what war had become by 1865—and without twenty-first-century distractions. Nearly 900 miles southwest of Richmond, on the east side of Mobile Bay, stand the best-preserved Civil War earthworks in the country. They crisscross the battlefield at Fort Blakely, Alabama—the same Fort Blakely where Sam Gaillard, Frye's great-grandfather, became a war prisoner for the second and final time in his Confederate military career. On this tract of forested land, now a state park, the last major battle of the Civil War occurred, a battle that needn't have happened at all.

The siege of Blakely came at the end of a swampy campaign that like the 1864 bloodbath in Virginia offered little in the way of glory. Most Americans are not even aware that it happened. Following Admiral David Farragut's success in the naval battle of Mobile Bay, which opened the lower reaches of the inlet to Northern forces in the summer of 1864 (this part of the story, at least, is well known thanks to Farragut's immortal exclamation, "Damn the torpedoes!"), Union strategists faced a dilemma. One of the last Confederate ports to remain unconquered—and a popular haven for blockade runners—the city of Mobile beckoned. But how to get there? Mines and underwater obstacles closed off the northern portion of the bay to all but the lightest Union ships, thereby preventing a naval assault. An overland operation on the western shore was also out of the question. Attacking Mobile from the south would mean contending with several belts of major fortifications and advancing across hostile territory without a reliable supply line.

Ultimately, none other than General William Tecumseh Sherman, who had enjoyed Mobile's hospitality prior to the war and knew the bay area well, suggested approaching the city from the east, and a plan emerged: While one Union force moved up the eastern shore, another would march diagonally from Pensacola, now a federal supply base, to Fort Blakely, part of a system of Confederate battlements constructed in anticipation of this very move. Here the two Union armies would join forces, annihilate the fort or force its surrender, and reach the city by crossing the Mobile-Tensaw River Delta, a maze of waterways that feed into the northern tip of the bay.

Grant's need for fresh bodies to make up for losses at places like the Wilderness and Cold Harbor delayed the Mobile campaign for months and almost led to its cancellation. But in the spring of 1865, with things going better in Virginia, the time finally seemed ripe for a renewed attack on what had come to be known as the "back door of the Confederacy."

From the start, it was a miserable operation. Reaching the Confederate earthworks meant days of marching in one of the soggiest, most humid places in North America. Days of battling mosquitoes, knee-deep bayous, venomous snakes, and the ever-present threat of Yellow Fever. Nevertheless, the Union forces, which included a number of African American units, made relatively rapid progress. On April 8, the Confederate defenses fell at Spanish Fort, an area just south of Blakely, and the two federal forces linked up as planned. Their combined strength, roughly 30,000 men, was simply too much for the fewer than 3,500 defenders of Fort Blakely, who had already spent more than a week fending off the Union column from Pensacola. The big battle came on April 9, and ended with a dramatic flourish as members of the 83rd Ohio Regiment, taking advantage of a ravine that shielded them from Confederate bullets and cannonballs, stormed Redoubt #4, the linchpin of the Southern defenses. With Union troops pouring over their earthworks, the Confederate garrison accepted defeat. Total casualties for both sides numbered somewhere around 3,500. What no one knew, of course, was that Lee had surrendered on this very same day, essentially ending the American Civil War. Like so much of the war—like any war, really—the Battle of Blakely didn't make much sense.

After the battle, Union troops allegedly forced the captured Confederate garrison to dig up the crude land mines that it had planted across various approaches to the fort. Sam Gaillard may have joined in that dangerous task along with everyone else—or perhaps, as an officer and a surgeon, he was spared. All we know for sure is that he was among the POWs sent to the Camp Massachusetts Prison on Ship Island, a desolate stretch of sand off the Mississippi coast. There, choked with hate, he would contend with African American guards, soldiers who were probably also veterans of the Battle of Blakely.

IN THE 1970S, AS middle-class whites fled from the urban core of Mobile and into suburbs on both sides of the bay, a savvy housing developer bought the Civil War battlefield at Spanish Fort and covered it with an afflu-ent bedroom community. Subdivisions now occupy most of the ground where gun emplacements and trenches were once dug. It's hard to think of any other place—even in suburb-packed northern Virginia—where Civil War history has been so ruthlessly blotted out. But just a few miles to the north, the Blakely battlefield remains as if frozen in time.

As likely to attract outdoorsmen as military-history buffs, it's a rug-ged spot—obviously a wretched place for a battle—with little of the remembrance apparatus usually featured at historic sites. The park has just two war memorials, both of recent construction. One commemorates the presence of Alabama troops in the fighting; the other, troops from Missouri. And that's it, apart from a few half-size cannons with plastic barrels. A drive on the gravel road that loops around the battlefield reveals a tough-looking landscape of scraggly pine flats, broken up here and there by brackish swamps and brush-covered ravines. It's a far cry from the elegant battlefield park at Shiloh or Gettysburg. But look closely and you'll see the tell-tale signs of nineteenth-century siege warfare—preserved here as nowhere else in the United States. Though weathered, Redoubt #4 still stands, opposite some Union earthworks, from which a New-England battery once engaged the Confederates in an artillery duel. The phantom outline of a zigzag trench stands out in the grass. And in what was once no-man's land, pits for skirmishers, looking like slightly larger versions of World-War-II-era foxholes, remain amazingly intact—as if their occupants have just left them. Imagine fortifications like these on a larger scale and you have the epic siege-scape where Lee and Grant became deadlocked outside Richmond and Petersburg.

Although this physical detritus of battle is fascinating, one feels a weight at Blakely comprised of more than just humidity. *Something*—a vague sense of embarrassment, perhaps?—hangs over the place. Certainly the Alabama legislature has shown little interest in insuring that the park's amazing earthworks survive another 150 years. The tiny staff at Blakely has had to make due with less and less state support, and rumors of the park's closure have become perennial. Some local whites assert (in private) that black legislators in Montgomery "won't vote to fund anything related to the Civil War." Other Bay area denizens, white and black alike, suggest that the significant role of African American units in the battle may have contributed to a lack of Southern interest in its commemoration.

Subterranean racial conflict often explains much that is otherwise inexplicable in the twenty-first-century Deep South. But the strange atmosphere at Blakely perhaps has far more to do with the disorienting effects of a battlefield left in its natural state—and the ambiguous nature of the event that the park feebly commemorates. We aren't accustomed to interpreting sites of Civil War memory without the guideposts offered by monuments, solemn rows of bronze cannons, and visitors' centers. And what kind of memory do we take away from Blakely, a battle fought by ignorant armies unaware that the war was already over? How do we fit this grotesquely ironic event into the grand narrative that usually ends with the surrender at Appomattox?

Frye's quest to understand what the American Civil War was *actually* like for his ancestors, his nimble parsing of myth and memory, creates a similarly unsettling effect. Little that he discovers fits the Lost Cause version of history that he inherited, like family china, from his Southern elders—a version that for better or worse lives with us still. Thus, as we read his remarkable book, we stand, in a sense, on the battlefield at Blakely, looking out on a landscape of war without familiar memorials and without familiar meanings.

ACKNOWLEDGMENTS

I am deeply indebted to other members of my family who carefully and lovingly preserved a written record of this momentous time in history. I'm particularly grateful to the descendants of Franklin Gaillard—his grandsons, Colonel Fred Gaillard and Charles Gaillard, and his granddaughter, Clair Gaillard Bissell—for copying and publishing Franklin's poignant letters in a 1941 volume entitled simply, *Franklin Gaillard's Civil War Letters*. Copies of those letters are also preserved in the Wilson Library at the University of North Carolina in Chapel Hill. Many of those letters, often in slightly abbreviated form, appear in this book. For serious students of Civil War history, the complete published collection of Franklin Gaillard's letters is still available in many libraries. I strongly recommend that fuller account.

Some of the letters here—two by Richebourg Gaillard and the first by Thomas Gaillard—also appeared in the excellent volume, *A World Turned Upside Down: The Palmers of the South Santee, 1818–1881*, edited by Louis P. Towles and published by the University of South Carolina Press. Caroline Gaillard Hurtel's family history, *The River Plantation of Thomas and Marianne Gaillard*, written in 1946 and published by the Rankin Press of Mobile, Alabama, contains one of Richebourg Gaillard's Civil War letters, and another written by Tom Palmer Gaillard just before his death at Port Hudson, Louisiana. The battlefield letter from Augusta Evans Wilson appeared in the winter 2011 edition of *Alabama Heritage* magazine. Other letters were handed down to me by my grandfather, Samuel Palmer Gaillard.

For perspective on the war, I reread portions of Shelby Foote's brilliant trilogy, *The Civil War*, as well as *I Rode with Stonewall*, by Henry Kyd Douglas, *A Stillness at Appomattox* by Bruce Catton, *Robert E. Lee: A Life* by Roy Blount Jr., and *Bloody Promenade: Reflections on a Civil War Battle* by Stephen Cushman.

Thanks once again to my wife, Nancy Gaillard, for her support and interest in this project; to my cousins, Palmer Hamilton and Tommy Gaillard; my colleague, Steven Trout, at the University of South Alabama; my editorial assistant, Rachael Fowler; and my editors and friends at NewSouth Books, Suzanne La Rosa and Randall Williams. I am grateful to all.

— FRYE GAILLARD

PART I

War and Memory

PROLOGUE

This is a story of the Civil War, as seen through the eyes of my own family. It is told, in part, through letters written by members of the family who either fought in the war or waited at home for news from the front. Some of these voices are full of idealism and hope; others, increasingly, are filled with gloom. Together, I think, they help paint a portrait of a horrifying time in American history, a time when 622,000 soldiers died on American soil, and when the southern half of the nation—so righteous and defiant when the conflict began—experienced a loss that was measured not only in blood but also in what one of my ancestors called the "cruelty and humiliation" of defeat.

I was struck as I read through the letters at how incongruously different generations have remembered those times. Perhaps my own generation was the last raised on stories of gallantry and courage, and admiration of the dashing generals who led our fighting men into battle and whose heroism was undiminished by defeat. Oddly, mine was also one of the

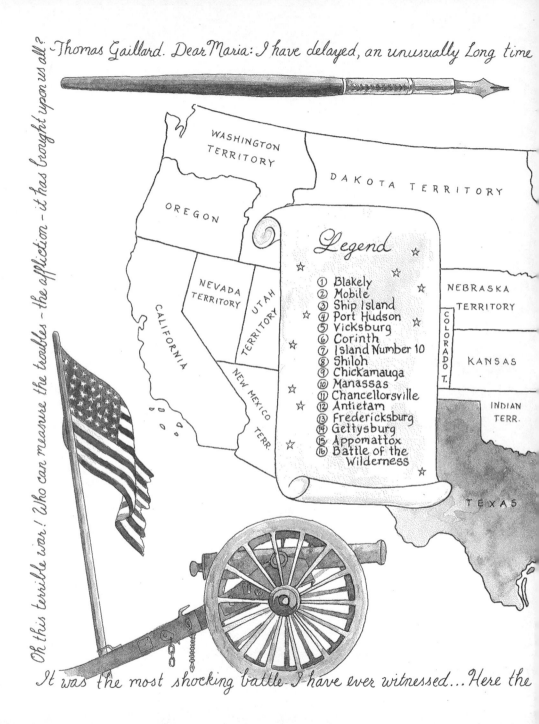

—Thomas Gaillard. Dear Maria: I have delayed, an unusually long time

Oh this terrible war! Who can measure the troubles — the affliction — it has brought upon us all?

It was the most shocking battle I have ever witnessed...Here the

Legend

1. Blakely
2. Mobile
3. Ship Island
4. Port Hudson
5. Vicksburg
6. Corinth
7. Island Number 10
8. Shiloh
9. Chickamauga
10. Manassas
11. Chancellorsville
12. Antietam
13. Fredericksburg
14. Gettysburg
15. Appomattox
16. Battle of the Wilderness

WASHINGTON TERRITORY

DAKOTA TERRITORY

OREGON

NEVADA TERRITORY

UTAH TERRITORY

CALIFORNIA

NEW MEXICO TERR.

NEBRASKA TERRITORY

COLORADO T.

KANSAS

INDIAN TERR.

TEXAS

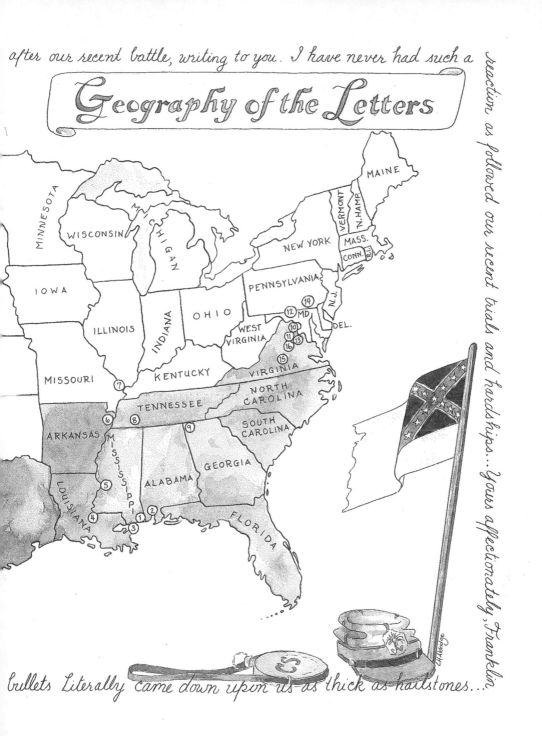

after our recent battle, writing to you. I have never had such a

Geography of the Letters

reaction as followed our recent trials and hardships... Yours affectionately, Franklin

bullets Literally came down upon us as thick as hailstones...

first generations to view the Civil War through the lens of civil rights—to see, often quite reluctantly, connections and flaws in Southern history that earlier generations couldn't bear to face. And so I have offered in Part I my own reflections on war and memory—on how the past lives on in the present, and how it draws us, slowly if we let it, in the painful direction of a more honest truth.

I.

STORIES AND QUESTIONS

M y grandfather, Samuel Palmer Gaillard, lived to be 103, and with his mind razor sharp until the end, he spent a lot of time reflecting on the past. This, to me, was understandable, for he had a lot of past on which to reflect. He was nine years old when the Civil War ended, and in 1956, when he was 100 and I was nine, he told me about the final days of it. There was one story in particular that I remember, an event he may have witnessed himself, but one that was, in any case, recorded by one of the members of his family.

It was April 1865 and the Southern army and the Southern landscape lay in ruins. In Monroe County, Alabama, where my grandfather's branch of the Gaillards lived, word quickly spread that Yankee soldiers were on their way. Soon, the clatter of hoofbeats sounded on the road, but it was not the Union Army after all. Not this time. It was, instead, a ragtag band of Confederates, heading south and running for their lives, doing their best to get away from the fighting.

"Where are you going, *running* from the Yankees," shouted Susan Frye Gaillard, my great-grandmother, as the Confederates galloped past her gate. "For heaven's sake go back and fight . . ."

I remember this story because it seemed so at odds with everything else I had learned about the war. Indeed, it was part of my Southern upbringing, as it was for so many in my generation, that the gallantry of the Confederate Army had never been tarnished by its defeat. I remember a book my father let me borrow, his personal copy of *I Rode with Stonewall*, written by Henry Kyd Douglas, who, as a young soldier barely in his twenties, served in Stonewall Jackson's brigade. Even now, I remember being stirred by the account in the second chapter of the book of Jackson earning his famous nickname. It was bestowed upon him at the first Battle of Bull Run, in the dying words of General B. E. Bee.

Douglas told the story this way:

. . . The storm swept toward us. Bee was back with his brigade but could not stay the onset. His horse was shot under him as he tried to rally and hold his men. At that supreme moment as if by inspiration, he cried out to them in a voice that the rattle of musketry could not drown, "Look! There is Jackson's brigade standing behind you like a stone wall!"

With these words of baptism as his last, Bee himself fell and died; and from that day left behind him a fame that will follow that of Jackson as a shadow.

This, to me, was the Civil War, the cornerstone of Southern pride, personified by a string of Southern generals whose qualities of courage were matched by their grace. The greatest of these, in the stirring canons of Confederate history—a history my family so deeply revered—was General Robert E. Lee. I met him first in Bruce Catton's *A Stillness at Appomattox*, again a book that I borrowed from my father, and later in Shelby Foote's *Civil War* trilogy, and in virtually every telling of the story, the greatness of Lee was beyond all dispute. In many ways, for me it still is, and why not? Here was a man who opposed secession, did not want the Civil War to happen, knew it was certain to be bloody and hard, and was prepared, in fact, to fight for the Union if Virginia had decided not to secede. But when Virginia made its fateful choice, Lee, as an honorable native son, made his as well.

He was, I later came to believe, a kind of Confederate Atticus Finch, a Southern archetype of duty and courage who came to his heroism with reluctance. He was indisputably bold as a general, keeping his adversaries off stride with his perpetual willingness to attack. But there was something else about him as well, some more subtle and elusive quality that lay, as far as my family was concerned, at the heart of Southern manhood. In his magnificent trilogy (which took him twenty years to complete, and he said he worked on it every single day), Shelby Foote set out to capture the character of Lee without descending completely into sentiment. I remember a passage about the Battle of Gettysburg, the historic moment when Lee overreached, when his own audacity served him badly. It was, most certainly, a turning point in the war, a three-day battle in which the dead and wounded totaled nearly 50,000, more than half from Lee's shrinking army.

From the back of Traveler, his familiar gray horse, Lee had watched the final charge up Cemetery Ridge, led by General George E. Pickett. When the Confederate advance was finally broken, and the survivors came streaming back across the valley, Lee rode gallantly out to meet them, offering, in the words of Shelby Foote, the kind of "solace and sustainment" that a father might offer to a grieving child.

"It's my fault," he declared, as he rode among them. "The blame is mine."

To the tearful general who commanded the charge, Lee, if anything, was even more tender. "Come, General Pickett," he said. "This has been my fight and upon my shoulders rests the blame. The men and officers of your command have written the name of Virginia as high today as it has ever been written before ... Your men have done all that men can do. The fault is entirely my own."

Such integrity and honor in a moment of defeat resonated powerfully with the members of my family, as with thousands of others, and buoyed by the bravery of Lee's fallen soldiers it lay at the heart of a history we revered. "For every Southern boy fourteen years old," William Faulkner wrote in 1948, "not once but whenever he wants it, there is the instant when it's still not yet two o'clock on the July afternoon in 1863 ... the furled flags are already loosened to break out and Pickett himself with his long oiled ringlets and his hat in one hand probably and his sword in the other looking up the hill waiting for Longstreet to give the word and it's all in the balance, it hasn't happened yet ..."

I remember some of those feelings myself, wishing, as only a boy might wish it, that we could somehow turn back the time, change the outcome, reward the valor in which we believed. It seems odd now, given the seismic shift of generations, but I remember gallops on the family farm, on a horse my uncle had named Jeb Stuart. Jeb, the horse, was high-stepping and fancy, a sorrel with some of the style, I knew, that had once belonged to his Civil War namesake. Indeed, Jeb, the general, was renowned for his dash—his red-lined cape and yellow sash, the ostrich plume he wore in his hat, and the bright red flower in his lapel. He was also legendary for his boldness, his cavalry raids behind the Union lines, gathering prisoners and critical intelligence as he rode, and I reveled in those moments on the farm when Jeb, the horse, and I would canter through the pastures, playing our private Civil War games.

And yet through it all—those years when this particular part of Southern history seemed so intertwined with the Southern present—there were other, more disconcerting voices that began to cast doubt on the glory of it all. In the beginning, what I heard most of all was my grandfather's voice. He had witnessed the end of the war himself, and in his memory it was anything but a childhood game. He had seen—or at least some people very close to him had—the ragtag band of Confederate soldiers running for their lives, ignoring the innocent pleas of his mother to go

The author's great-grandfather, Samuel Septimus Gaillard, left, and grandfather, S. P. Gaillard.

back and fight. He had seen the victorious Union cavalry pouring through his part of southern Alabama, and he had heard the stories of his war-weary father, Samuel Septimus Gaillard.

Sam, like his older brother, Edmund, was a Confederate surgeon, and that was one of the worst jobs you could have. The field hospitals were dreadful places, particularly in the aftermath of a battle—overwhelmed by legions of the wounded, groaning, begging for water or some kind of relief, screaming with the amputation of their limbs. Blood and body parts seemed to be everywhere, and disease fell cruelly upon the maimed. But for Sam Gaillard, all of that was only a part of his misery, for he had also suffered even more directly. He was wounded at the Battle of Vicksburg, and then taken prisoner by the Union army. Promptly released in a prisoner exchange, he was captured again near the end of the war, and sent to a prison camp on Ship Island.

The island was little more than a long spit of sand, one of several off the Mississippi coast that served as a barrier during hurricanes. For Sam Gaillard, it was a desolate place, hot and barren with a handful of twisted oaks and pines, offering only the most pitiful shade from the blinding force of the afternoon sun. There was a wooden stockade on the western end of the island, and a few meager huts amid the bone-colored dunes. But as Sam told his family, and as my grandfather later told me, the worse part of his confinement was the cruelty of the guards. They were black men, first of all, Negro soldiers who were happy to fight for their own freedom, and who had little sympathy for these Confederate rebels, who had, after all, gone to war for the right to own slaves.

Sam later told the members of his family that the prisoners were prodded and jabbed with bayonets, a few even shot, when they moved too slow. His memories grew more sullen with time, becoming a part of the family lore, and the retribution by the Negro troops became a microcosm of defeat.

As a boy I never knew what to make of these stories. What was it, really, that my grandfather was saying? I admit it took years to sort through the layers, but even at the time there was something unsettling about war and memory and what seemed to be an obvious swirl of contradiction. Was the Civil War truly, as I had so often heard, a time of gallantry undiminished by loss? Were the integrity of Lee, the dash of Jeb Stuart, and the ferocious tenacity of Stonewall Jackson really the defining truths of the story? Or was there something more ugly and painful?

Later, of course, I would wonder about the racial overtones of it, but even before that difficult time, before the civil rights movement of the 1960s recast our whole understanding of history, I was a little unsure how to think about the war. Why did my hundred-year-old grandfather, who had lived through the end of it as a child, hold a view more dismal than that of my father, who had loaned me his books and regaled me with stories about Robert E. Lee? Why did this much older man seem so somber, perhaps even bitter, about what had happened in the South, while so many others gloried in the past?

Part of the answer, I would soon learn, lay in the terrible scale of the numbers—the tally of the dead and the wounded and maimed—a tragedy of monumental proportions. But why, then, if all that were true, was the whole adventure such a fierce source of pride?

I puzzled over this in my early teens, the contradictions between the glory and the pain, and then I more or less moved on. By the time I reached my college years, I was fully caught up in the Southern present, the melodrama over black and white, as civil rights replaced Civil War at what seemed to be the core of our Southern identity. It was only later—nearly thirty years later—that I again began to think about the connection.

2

LETTERS AND GUNS

n the early 1990s, as I was working on a family memoir later published
under the title, *Lessons from the Big House*, I came upon a cache of
Civil War letters. Some were written by Thomas Gaillard, my great-
great-grandfather and family patriarch who lived in Mobile. In the 1830s,
Thomas had moved his family to Alabama, making the overland trek
from South Carolina to a sprawling plantation on the Alabama River.
Before the move Thomas had been a state legislator, and in that position,
had established himself as a Southern moderate, a man who believed in
state's rights, as so many Southerners said they did, but one who also
hoped against hope that the South could avoid a war with the North.

It was true that Thomas was a Southern patriot, a man who had made
his peace with slavery—how else could he work his 8,000 acres?—and
who shared the widely held belief that the South was heir to the American
Revolution. It was the South, after all, that was threatened with invasion
as the winds of war began to stir. But Thomas was worried about four of
his six sons. Peter, the youngest, was deaf, and thus mercifully unsuited
to military service, and John, the oldest, had died in a curious hunting
accident not too long before the guns at Fort Sumter. He was out shooting ducks on a winter day, standing for hours in the frigid water, and a

strange paralysis began to set in. Instead of abating in the warmth of his home, the numbness grew worse, until, eventually, it simply consumed him. John died at the age of forty-six.

Then came the war, and on the day that Alabama seceded, Thomas put a row of candles in his window. In retrospect, it seemed a curious show of support, measured and somber, but how could it have been otherwise? Having turned seventy, Thomas was too old for war. He had given up his river plantation in Monroe County, hoping for a quiet life in Mobile, and suddenly he had four sons in the fight.

Samuel Septimus, Richebourg, and Edmund had all been assigned to the western front, where it soon became clear that the news was never good. The Mississippi River and its massive tributaries offered an easy path of invasion for the Union army under Ulysses Grant, and Thomas was fatalistic from the start.

"This will be a sanguinary and merciless war," he wrote in May 1861. "The invasion is one of the Goths and the Vandals . . ."

One member of the family who did not share Thomas's gloom was his younger son, Franklin, who, in many ways, was the family firebrand. Franklin was thirty-two when the war began, a Southern patriot who believed a Confederate victory was at hand. He looked the part of a planter's son, erect and sandy-haired like his father, though with a more sunken and angular face perhaps not as handsome. He had spent his boyhood in Alabama but returned to the Carolinas for his schooling. In 1849, he graduated first in his class at the College of South Carolina and soon became a newspaper editor. First for the *Winnsboro Register* and then the *Daily South Carolinian*, he beat the drum for secession and war—yearning, he said, for the day when "our country shall be free of the despotism which these Northern people now hang over our devoted heads . . ."

Franklin Gaillard, standing between his wife, Tattie, and niece, Catherine, the daughter of John Gaillard. Seated in front are Franklin's sisters, Lydia, Betsy, and Nan.

As his writings made clear, Franklin rarely thought in shades of gray. He joined the Confederate army eager for the fight, and for nearly four years, kept a steady correspondence with his family, assuring those back home that "the Yankees will cave in . . ." That was certainly his view early on, and now a hundred and fifty years later, his letters are an elegant chronicle of war.

His fateful journey as a soldier began with Fort Sumter and carried him bravely through some of the major battles of the war. The first was Bull Run, which was, for Franklin, a triumph as decisive as he could imagine. In a letter to his father soon after the fighting, he described the rout of the Union Army: "They left artillery, small arms, muskets, rifles, coats, blankets, provisions and everything."

The skirmishing leading up to that moment began on July 18, 1861, and three days later, as the showdown loomed less than fifty miles from the nation's capital, so confident were the Union forces of victory that many members of Congress came out to watch. They brought their ladies and their picnic lunches and parked their carriages on a nearby hill. But their gaiety quickly turned to horror as the Confederates staged a bayonet charge, having been urged by their leader, Stonewall Jackson, to "yell like furies." It was the first time in the war that the rebel yell would ring through the fields, and the Union soldiers, still largely untrained, panicked at the sound.

Franklin Gaillard was in the middle of it. With the 2nd South Carolina Regiment, where he would soon earn the rank of lieutenant colonel, he raced down a hill and past the stream that was known as Bull Run, fighting not only the enemy in blue but also his fear and finally his fatigue, as the horrors of the scene unfolded all around him.

"You can form no idea," he wrote to his father, "of the thirst created by the excitement and fatigue of battle. The indifference with which one regards the dead and wounded is another astonishing feature. After . . . the enemy had been driven off, I began to gather the canteens of the enemy for our own famishing men who could not leave ranks. The first I got containing water was on a dead man. The side of the canteen was bathed in blood up to the very mouth . . . . My thirst was so great that regardless of this I turned it so the water would run out at the bloodless side, emptied it into my own and drank it. Before I went into battle the very sight of the blood of a dead man would have caused me to shudder. After our own men had been provided for I gave water to several of the wounded enemy. They seemed very grateful and were surprised at our kindness—it was so different from what their lying generals had represented to them. The battle sounded terrible but the destruction of life was not nearly so great as would have been supposed from the sound. The moral effect of the victory can not well be calculated. It has thrown confusion into the ranks of the enemy and in spite of the confident and defiant resolution of their Congress, has involved the whole object of the war in doubt and distrust. I feel very hopeful that next spring will end the contest and bring a recognition of our independence. It may come before that time."

FOR A WHILE, MANY shared that view. Even Jefferson Davis, president of the newly formed Confederacy, permitted himself a few moments of hope. Davis had always understood the odds, understood that the Southern forces would be outnumbered, and that Northern factories could equip the Union army much better than the one it would soon oppose. Knowing this, Davis had worked hard to frame the debate, to craft an argument for Southern independence that would stir not only the people of the South, but perhaps also touch the conscience of the North.

"All we ask," he declared, "is to be let alone."

Like his counterpart, Abraham Lincoln—whom he so oddly resembled with his high cheekbones and deep, gaunt features, as if the strain of the war were already painted across his face—Davis was a man of stirring eloquence. He regarded leadership as a sacred trust, and in the days leading up to the First Battle of Bull Run (or Manassas, as it was often called in the South), he fretted at the scarcity of news from the front. Finally, on a Sunday, as the armies were taking their places for the fight, he set out from Richmond, the Confederate capital, traveling first by train and then horseback, directly into the teeth of the battle. On he rode through the smoke and the noise, rallying the Southern forces on the way. If the day were lost and the Northern troops broke through, he wanted to share that moment with the men. But when the battle turned the other way, when the Union soldiers broke and ran, Davis himself galloped into the chase and reveled in the flush of Confederate triumph.

His only regret was that the Southern army was so exhausted that it made no sense—particularly in the sudden rainstorm that followed—to press an immediate attack on Washington.

There would be time enough for that. The message from the battlefield was emphatic, and those who had seen the fighting for themselves had little doubt about what it was. The Southern army would fight. It would attack with a fury that the Northern forces would be hard-pressed to match, for in the North they were fighting not in immediate defense of their homes, but rather for something much more abstract—for the idea of *union*, the belief that the country should not be divided—and if the cost in blood was to be high, the inevitable question would be whether it was worth it. In the startling summer of 1861, in the first bloody rush of Northern defeat, some thought the answer was already clear.

"So short lived has been the American Union," wrote a reporter from the London *Times* in the immediate aftermath of Bull Run, "that men who saw its rise may live to see its fall."

3.

NEWS FROM THE FRONT

Down in Alabama, Thomas Gaillard was not so sure. He had heard the same assessment from his own son, Franklin, but Thomas by nature was not an optimist. The experience of life had taught him otherwise. During his younger days in South Carolina, when he took his place in the state legislature, he could see the looming dangers of division. Even as early as the 1820s he had begun to worry about civil war, and though he blamed the meddlesome people of the North, at least primarily, he never quite shared in the righteous fervor—really a kind of sullen petulance—rising all around him in the South.

It was true that Thomas supported slavery, having made his uneasy peace, and he resented the condemnations by Northern abolitionists, who simply didn't understand the Southern way of life. Still, he knew the nation had been forged in blood, and in the legislature of South Carolina he served as a member of the Unionist Party. He argued against the theory of "nullification," a notion put forward by John C. Calhoun, the most powerful politician in South Carolina, who believed that since the states had entered the union voluntarily, they could, if they chose, simply refuse to abide by its laws. Calhoun had proposed the theory in 1828, responding to a tariff passed by Congress that was unpopular with the cotton states of the South. But everybody knew that this was merely a shot across the bow—a warning that the South would tear the union apart if its interests were infringed, especially by an assault on slavery.

Standing against those passions, Thomas Gaillard lost by a margin of two to one when he ran for reelection in 1830. Soon after that defeat he moved his family to Alabama. By 1861, he had come to a reluctant support of secession, but from all accounts he was not surprised when news from the war began to turn sour. In Virginia, where Franklin Gaillard

Thomas and Marianne Gaillard, the author's great-great-grandparents.

was fighting under Robert E. Lee, there seemed to be some hope. But in the west, Thomas thought the outlook was grim. Early in 1862, Union forces led by Ulysses Grant swept into Tennessee, winning victories at Fort Henry and Fort Donelson, as they prepared to move south into Mississippi. In Thomas's mind the turning point was Shiloh, a two-day battle in western Tennessee where the 23,000 killed, wounded or captured in forty-eight hours were greater than the combined casualties in all the wars the United States had ever fought—the American Revolution, the War of 1812, and the Mexican War. In the end, the Confederates were forced to retreat, but the death toll was worse on the Union side, and for General Grant, who was never averse to the shedding of blood, the lesson of the terrible battle was clear. "I gave up the idea," he said, "of saving the Union except by complete conquest."

Upon hearing the news, Thomas Gaillard, a gentle man with sons who were now in Grant's line of fire, wrote an anguished letter to his family:

Oh this terrible war! Who can measure the troubles—the affliction—it has brought upon us all? It has pleased the Almighty to inflict upon us this severe chastisement—and it is our duty to submit in Christian spirit . . . We can not foresee His ultimate purpose in thus scourging our people with the direst of calamities. But even in the depth of our sorrow, we can also see a glimmering of mercy . . .

The contest is fast approaching a crisis, and I am not sorry for it. The sooner it is brought to an issue the better . . . Let His will be done.

THOMAS DIDN'T LIVE TO see the answer to his prayers. What he saw instead in the remaining two years of his life was suffering and blood on a scale that he had never imagined. The cannons were bigger, the guns more accurate, and though the soldiers were indisputably brave, their gallantry often simply turned into carnage. To make it even worse, the

South was losing. On April 29, 1862, three weeks after the Battle of Shiloh, Admiral David Farragut seized the port of New Orleans for the Union, and the Northern army under Grant moved toward the Mississippi town of Corinth. Their strategic goal was to seize control of the Mississippi River and thus to cut the Confederacy in two.

As the casualties mounted, they eventually, inevitably touched the Gaillard family. On April 7, just as the Battle of Shiloh was ending, Thomas's third son, Richebourg, was captured at a place called Island Number Ten, a swampy spit of land in the Mississippi River between the borders of Tennessee and Missouri. Richebourg's garrison surrendered there without a fight, and from his prison quarters at Camp Chase, Ohio, he wrote a despairing letter to one of his brothers (misspelling his name).

Dear Edmond

. . . You all no doubt feel chagrined at the misfortune which has befallen the 1st Ala Regiment. We were taken without the firing of a gun. If we were sacrificed for the good of the Army at Corinth, all well; but if we were neglected by our superiors with no such purpose, then there is nothing to console us . . . We were surrendered eight hours before any of us knew it. How long we will be prisoners, God only knows. I am restricted. Remember me to all . . .

Your brother, R. Gaillard

Richebourg, as it happened, was quickly exchanged and rejoined the Confederate army at Port Hudson, Louisiana, where Edmund's son, Tom Palmer, was stationed. According to a story told sadly in the family (I remember hearing it from one of my aunts more than ninety years after it happened), Tom Palmer, an impetuous boy of nineteen, would climb the Confederate fortifications just to see what the Yankees were doing. More seasoned soldiers warned him against it, but Tom Palmer was brash and refused to listen, and finally a Union sniper shot him dead.

He was merely one of the first to fall along that particular stretch of the Mississippi River. Three hundred miles north at the port of Vicksburg, Confederate forces hunkered down amid heavily fortified bluffs and ra-vines. Sam Gaillard was there, promoted now to captain, and as far as we know he shared in the momentary surge in morale as the Southern army, at least temporarily, beat back the attacks of Grant and his men. From Corinth to Jackson, Union troops had swept across Mississippi, winning fight after fight, but now at Vicksburg the tide seemed to turn. On May 19 and again on May 22, 1863, Union assaults ended quite literally in a bloody mess when the Southern entrenchments were simply too strong. But Vicksburg and the town of Port Hudson represented the South's final hold on the river, and if frontal assaults for the moment didn't work Grant and his army settled in for a siege.

Hour after hour for the next six weeks, the Northern artillery bombarded Vicksburg, reducing so many of its houses to rubble that many of the citizens began living in caves. "Some of these were quite commodious," wrote historian Shelby Foote, "with several rooms, and the occupants brought in chairs and beds and even carpets to add to the comfort, sleeping soundly or taking dinner unperturbed while the world outside seemed turned to flame and thunder." But the time soon came when there was almost nothing left to eat, when the defenders and citizens of Vicksburg had consumed all the beef and pork and most of the grain within the city's defenses, and the army was forced to eat mules. Scurvy and other sickness quickly swept through the troops, and by the end of June half the garrison had fallen ill. By July 4, the Confederates could hold out no longer, and General John Pember-ton, their beleaguered commander, surrendered his troops to General Grant. Sam Gaillard was one of those taken prisoner, having also been wounded in the shoulder. Five days later Sam's brother, Richebourg, was once again a prisoner as well, when Southern forces at Port Hudson surrendered, giving the Northern army under Grant total control of the Mississippi River.

"The Father of Waters," President Lincoln declared, "again goes unvexed to the sea."

For Thomas Gaillard, waiting in Mobile, the news from the East was not any better. He had been relieved to learn in the autumn of 1862 that Franklin had survived the Battle of Antietam, or Sharpsburg, as it was also known. That particular fight, on September 17, 1862, was almost as bloody as the Battle of Shiloh, with total casualties of 22,717. More than 10,000 of the killed, wounded or missing came from the ranks of the Confederate army, and Thomas could only give thanks that Franklin was not among that number. In December, however, Franklin was shot in the face at Fredericksburg, a battle won by the South. He remained out of action until Chancellorsville the following spring, returning just in time to fight in another stirring victory for Lee.

But then came Gettysburg. It was a defeat for the Confederacy that was all the more stunning because it happened one day before the surrender at Vicksburg, and because the cost in blood was so high. In a letter to his family, this is the way Franklin Gaillard described it:

The Battle of Gettysburg was, I think, the most sanguinary of the war and was as clear a defeat as our army ever met with. Our Brigade suffered very severely . . . . We were, in ten minutes time or less, terribly butchered. A body of infantry to our left opened on us; and as a volley of grape would strike our line, I saw half a dozen at a time knocked up and flung to the ground like trifles. In about that short space of time we had about half our men killed or wounded. It was the most shocking battle I have ever witnessed. There were familiar forms and faces with parts of their heads shot away, legs shattered, arms torn off, etc. . . . The enemy's infantry came up and we stood within thirty steps of each other. They loaded and fired deliberately. I never saw more stubbornness.

It was so desperate I took two shots with my pistol at men scarcely thirty steps from me. I could not see that I did any damage but there were some seven or eight dead lying just about where I was shooting. . . . We charged upon the party opposed to us and drove them pell-mell through the woods, shooting them down and taking prisoners at every step. We pursued them to the foot of the stone mountain, the strongpoint of their position, where we attacked them. Here the bullets literally came down upon us as thick as hailstones. It is scarcely necessary to say we fell back . . . .

The battle was an unfortunate one. Our army went into it in magnificent style and I never saw it fight better but the position defeated us. For this I blame our Generals . . . It was caused by their overconfidence. The greatest misfortune is that it destroyed the unbounded confidence reposed in Gen. Lee. Before, the army believed he could not err. They now see that he can . . . .

For Franklin Gaillard, the fighting would continue, kindled by the stubborn belief that if the South could just hold on a little longer, perhaps the North would grow weary of the fight. That was the hope, the article of faith, that helped keep him going.

But a fateful battle lay just ahead . . .

4.

THE WILDERNESS

On February 27, 1864, Franklin wrote one of the saddest letters of his life, affirming his receipt of the news that his father, Thomas Gaillard, had died. "I am satisfied that there is no living being who can point to anything mean or little in his character or disposition," Franklin wrote to his sister, Lydia. "His rule of action was so near that of the Christian Philosopher as humanity could practice it. His want of success in worldly matters I attribute solely to this source."

Even in the midst of these tender lines, tucked gracefully between them, there seemed to be a trace of Franklin's ambivalence toward a man who moved so gently in the world. As Franklin understood clearly, his father had lived a life that was shadowed by failure. First as a politician Thomas stood quietly, at least for a time, against the passions that would lead to civil war, and for that stand he would experience the sting of political defeat. As a planter his fortunes rose and fell. And even as a scholar, which he became in the middle stages of his life, he was occasionally unhappy with his own work. But through it all, he lived with a kind of fatalistic integrity, a patrician's grace, that even a brash young man like Franklin admired.

Franklin, however, was cut from different cloth. Having lobbied for secession, and thus for war, he was still determined to win. "That we have received staggering blows there is no disguising," he wrote to his family in South Carolina. "But they are such that we can recover from—for the enemy suffered severely in inflicting them."

His resolve was buoyed—grimly—by the Battle of Chickamauga on September 19–20, 1863. General Lee had sent a part of his army, including General Joseph Kershaw's Brigade, in which Franklin now served as a colonel, to shore up the forces of General Braxton Bragg, who was bracing for a fight in northern Georgia. This was mountainous, thickly wooded terrain where confusion reigned in the course of the battle, but the Union army under William Rosecrans was driven from the field. In the mounting catalogue of death and carnage that became the central reality of the war—Shiloh, Antietam, Gettysburg—only Gettysburg was worse than Chickamauga. And though victorious, the Southern army suffered more than the North's with more than 18,000 killed, wounded or missing.

Franklin's letters home began to show traces of battle fatigue: "When the terrible excitement of battle was over it took me a week or more to recover from the depression . . . I saw shot down around me some of the finest men in the regiment." But there was also a bittersweet flicker over a chance encounter with his older brother, Sam.

I met right face to face with Sam who was hunting for me. The meeting you may know was no less pleasant than surprising. He was going one way and I another so we could not be together more than half an hour. It was a great disappointment to have to part with him so soon . . . He is heartily sick of war. He is the most domestic member of the family. Never troubled himself much about public matters and could always find enough to engage him at home. His children he says cannot understand why he does not remain with them and that seems to worry him. . . .

The brothers never saw each other again. Sam, having been paroled after his capture at Vicksburg, fought for a time in east Tennessee and northern Georgia before his unit moved south to the Alabama coast. Franklin once again headed north, rejoining the army of Robert E. Lee in time for a battle that took its name, not from a town or a mountain or a stream, but simply from the nature of the terrain. The Battle of the Wilderness was, by nearly any measure, one of the most brutal of the war. General Grant, flush from success in the western theater, had taken overall command of the Union army, and President Lincoln, it seemed, was finally satisfied with his choice. Lincoln had run through a handful of generals, and none of the others—not McDowell, not McClellan, not even George Meade, the Union victor at Gettysburg—inspired the same confidence as Grant. Whatever his reputed lack of refinement, and despite the alcoholic demons that raged in his soul, Grant some-how seemed to have what it took. He was rougher and more aggressive, willing to fight a war of attrition if that's what was needed against Lee's fierce, but smaller army.

IN MAY 1864, GRANT's resolve—and Lincoln's—would be put to the test in a tangled, scrub-oak thicket in Virginia, a "jungle," in the words of Shelby Foote. In his book, *Bloody Promenade*, Virginia author Stephen Cushman quoted from the journal of Katherine Couse, a woman who lived near the edge of the Wilderness, perilously close to the fighting. Describing the mounting horror of the conflict, Couse wrote:

  . . . it is soul sickening to listen to the continual crack of small arms, then the loud resounding cannon, shell whizzing, balls whistling, soldiers yelling and hollowing as they rush on Oh! God human beings killing each other. This wicked war will it never come to an end.

The three-day battle began May 5, 1864, and despite the massive numerical odds—122,000 troops under Grant, compared with 65,000 under Lee—the Southern general was eager to attack. He sent his men along three different roads that tunneled through the tangled canopy of trees. Soon the fighting became frantic and confused, and friendly fire—that famous oxymoron of war—took a massive toll on both sides. One who fell was James Longstreet, one of Lee's most capable generals, who was shot through the neck and carried from the battlefield on a stretcher. He was still giving orders as he left, raising his hat in salute to his men, who cheered in reply.

Longstreet was luckier than some, for there were places in this terrible terrain where the fighting became so fierce, and the heat from the artillery barrage was so intense, that the jungle simply erupted in flames. The fire surged quickly through the infestations of briers, and many of the wounded were burned alive when the blaze spread faster than they could crawl.

Franklin Gaillard died the second day. Mercifully enough, he was not burned alive. He died from a bullet and death came quickly, and from all accounts brought genuine grief to the men of his command. "What his loss is to us of the brigade as an officer and as a man it is impossible to overestimate," wrote his cousin, W. P. DuBose. "It would gratify his friends to see how deep and universal the feeling has been and how irreparable his loss is regarded."

Back in Alabama, his sister Lydia pulled out the last letter she had received, the one Franklin wrote about the death of their father, and she penned a simple inscription on the bottom: "Last letter received from my dear brother who was killed at the battle of Wilderness." In another margin, his younger sister, Marianne, was more philosophical: "Poor Frank was killed at the battle of the Wilderness in Va. a few weeks after writing this. He little thought then that his brave and noble spirit would soon join those who had gone before. Such is life. What is it compared with eternity?"

BUT THE WAR WENT on. Richebourg Gaillard languished in a Union prisoner of war camp, and his brother Sam labored miserably in a Confederate hospital north of Mobile. In Virginia, meanwhile, General Grant kept coming. Despite casualties that would soon approach 60,000, he made good on a promise, delivered in writing to Abraham Lincoln: "Whatever happens, there will be no turning back."

Eventually, it was simply too much. On April 9, 1865, Lee surrendered to Grant at Appomattox, and after it was over Grant reflected wistfully upon his foe and upon an ending long overdue:

As he was a man of such dignity, with an impassable face, it was impossible to say whether he felt inwardly glad that the end had finally come, or felt sad over the result and was too manly to show it. Whatever his feelings they were entirely concealed from my observation; but my own feelings, which had been quite jubilant upon receipt of his letter, were sad and depressed. I felt like anything rather than rejoicing at the downfall of a foe who had fought so long and so valiantly, and had suffered so much for a cause, though that cause was, I believe, one of the worst for which a people ever fought.

Even after that nobility of surrender, and whatever relief it may have brought, the fighting continued—little skirmishes scattered throughout the South, and Samuel Septimus Gaillard, perhaps the most war-weary of the brothers, suffered till the end. On April 9, the day of Appomattox, Sam was taken prisoner at the Battle of Fort Blakely, captured in the swamplands north of Mobile. He was taken from there to Ship Island off the Mississippi coast where his torment at the hands of Negro guards—his feelings of humiliation and defeat—became a part of the family identity.

Writing about it nearly ninety years later, and about the years of Reconstruction that followed, Sam's son and my grandfather, Samuel Palmer Gaillard, could not, even then, conceal the bitterness of the memory.

Samuel Septimus Gaillard . . . was again captured at the fall of Fort Blakely on Mobile Bay and was among those prisoners that suffered cruelty and humiliation on Ship Island, near Biloxi, Mississippi, at the hands of colored troops. . . . History shows that emancipation at the point of the bayonet was enforced and followed by an unreasoning bitterness exceeding that visited upon our alien foes in modern warfare. Reconstruction and Freedman's Bureau, enforced by soldier's bayonets, left a bitter taste in my mouth. I, S. P. Gaillard, saw it.

5

LAYERS OF MEMORY

F or every succeeding generation, it seems, at least for the next hundred years or so, and perhaps even now, the memories of the war were there for the taking. For my grandfather, who was too young to fight but lived through some of the history himself, every recollection was raw and immediate and remained that way for the rest of his life. But for my Southern family, and for many others, the generations that followed set out gamely to soften the edges, searching for the heroism and the goodness, refuting the notion of General Grant that the South had simply been in the wrong.

Among my relatives, one of those most active in shaping our memory was Caroline Gaillard Hurtel—"Cousin Oline," as we called her in the family. In 1946, the year I was born, she wrote a book called *The River Plantation*, telling the story of her great-grandfather, Thomas Gaillard. She ended her history with the Civil War, and amid her affirmations of "gallantry"—a word I heard so often growing up—she offered two stories that lay at the heart of what she believed. They were stories of loss, to be sure, but they were also filled with pride.

One was about a young man named Billie Gaillard, a grandson of Thomas, who went off to fight at the age of seventeen and apparently spent most of his time in the army dodging sniper bullets as a sentry.

When his unit was overrun in 1865, he avoided capture because he was hospitalized with malaria. He was in Columbus, Mississippi, when the fighting finally stopped, when his Confederate commanders decided at last, fully a month after Appomattox, that they might as well quit. Billie set out for home after that, trudging along the back roads of the South, dead broke and hungry, heading in the general direction of Mobile.

Not long ago, I picked up my copy of *The River Plantation* and reread the account of Billie's journey, remembering also the deserter's odyssey of W. P. Inman, a character in the novel *Cold Mountain*. In that best-seller from 1997, Inman, the anti-hero of the tale, is war-weary and wounded, desperate only to make his way home, willing, in fact, to endure any pain in the hope of reuniting with the woman he loves. I found myself wondering even more about Billie. Was his journey in any way the same? Was he lonely and afraid? Did he carry in his heart the agony of the Confederate defeat?

Not according to *The River Plantation*. Billie, instead, made it safely to Mobile, where he hitched a ride upriver to the family plantation in Claiborne, Alabama. His boat was crowded with Union soldiers who treated him kindly, giving him food and a place to sleep, and when they came to Claiborne Landing, Billie leapt gracefully ashore.

As the packet steamed on up the river, the young Confederate, his spirit still undefeated, waved good-bye to the men in blue. Then he eagerly began the ascent of the three hundred and sixty-five steps that climbed the steep wooden bluff to the little town of Claiborne. He was whistling. The war was over and he was home.

It may have happened exactly that way. Billie Gaillard, at the age of nineteen, may have been swept away in a sudden contentment, happy just to be back in Alabama. Certainly, it was clear that Cousin Oline found some peace in that understanding, just as she did in another story handed down in the family. This one, which she also recounts in *The River Plantation*, is sadder than the story of Billie's last march, more obviously filled with a certain kind of pathos. It is the story of one of the Gaillard women, who confronted the end of the war on her own.

Caroline Gaillard, before the surrender at Appomattox, when her family members knew that the war was lost, decided that the time had come to sell her slaves. Caroline was a widow. Her husband John had died before the war, and Caroline knew she would need the money—she asked, in fact, for payment in gold—if she were to survive the wreckage of defeat. But when her first slave mounted the auction block, a kind-hearted woman whose name was Hannah, Caroline knew she could not do it. In the pages of *The River Plantation*, this is the way the moment unfolded.

When Caroline saw the tears rolling down her slave's dark cheeks, she impulsively went up on the block, and putting her arms around Hannah, they wept together. Then Caroline looked at faithful old Bina; at Uncle George, who through the perilous days of the war had been her helper and protector. She noticed other weeping slaves, and marked the troubled face of Uncle Dick, who had taken several cows to Mobile, selling milk that his mistress might have bread. Then deeply touched by their grief, she went quietly to the auctioneer and called off the sale. . . . Caroline was left penniless.

I SUPPOSE WHEN I first read the story as a boy, this is the way I wanted to see it, the bitterness gentled, the motives made pure. Indeed, what my cousin had done with this memory must have soothed the conscience of a whole generation. I don't mean that she did it alone. For nearly a century after the war, certainly for the first eighty years, there was a barrage of this kind of writing, reaching its pinnacle in *Gone with the Wind*. The cornerstone of our collective understanding was that the South was never wrong, not fundamentally and never in its heart, and scattered through the ashes of Southern defeat was something too proud and precious to die.

But memories can crumble against the forces of time, especially those that are fragile at the core. And the psyche of the South, so rooted in the past, proved to be more fragile than most. I remember being surprised by this, for the illusions, after all, had been so elaborate, such a complex tangle of history and myth, prejudice and pride; and the Civil War, somehow, was the key to it all. If we could make something glorious out of our defeat, and out of the terrible cost in blood, then maybe we could live with the other pieces, too—that legacy of slavery and segregation and oppression, that denial of humanity toward a people whose humanity was all too clear.

One of the bravest Southern writers to unravel this knot was Lillian Smith, who in 1949 published a book called *Killers of the Dream*. I read it first in the 1960s when the civil rights movement was sweeping through the South, and the effect of Smith's elegant and poetic prose was to add some layers to my understanding, a context for the passions of the hour. Writing about the Civil War and its aftermath, and about the depth of Southern hurt, this was a part of what Smith had to say:

Then the war came. And the South lost everything it cherished. And for a little while there was no room for hate in most men's hearts, for there was so much sadness. The whole region mourned its dead, its loss, its deep hurt.

For a time, said Smith, the South did its best to soothe the pain by heaping glory on its memory of the dead, and the Civil War became a lost and noble cause. In the end, however, the illusion didn't work, not in our collective heart of hearts, and the hurt gave way to something worse—to a vast dishonesty driven by guilt, and obscured by a desperate love of the past. Lillian Smith explained it this way, our dirty Southern secret, hidden only from ourselves and tied so inextricably to the war:

The South grew more sensitive to criticism, more defensive and dishonest in its thinking. For deep down in their hearts, southerners knew they were wrong. They knew it in slavery just as they . . . know today that segregation is wrong. It was not only the North's criticism that made them defensive, it was their own conscience. Our grandparents called themselves Christians and sometimes believed they were. Believing it, they were compelled to believe it was morally right for them to hold slaves. They could not say, 'We shall keep our slaves because they are profitable, regardless of right and wrong.' A few tough old realists who didn't claim to be in the Fold probably did say it. But to most, such words would have seemed as fantastic as a confession of their mixed reasons for opposing slavery would have seemed to the Yankees. Our grandfathers' conscience compelled them to justify slavery and they did: by making the black man 'different,' setting him outside God's law, reducing him to less than human. In a way that would have seemed blasphemous, had they stopped to think, they took God's place and 'decided' which of His creatures have souls and which do not. And once doing it, they continued doing it, and their sons continued doing it, and their grandsons, telling themselves and their children more and more and more lies about white superiority until they no longer knew the truth and were lost in a maze of fantasy and falsehood that had little resemblance to the actual world they lived in.

It's a strange thing how a man's own conscience can trap his soul.

AFTER I READ SMITH's essay while caught in the currents of the 1960s, my own understanding of the Civil War—my inherited memory of it, so to speak—began to peel back one layer at a time, more or less in reverse chronological order. I knew that the present was tied to that past. You could see it on the dome of the Alabama Capitol, where George Wallace flew the Confederate flag as he launched his defense of "segregation forever." You could hear it in the rhetoric of every Southern politician who, in all the turbulence of the civil rights years, compared the federal troops required to keep order with the invading armies of a hundred years before. Slowly, in an ironic way, many of us who supported civil rights followed the example of Southern demagogues in our new understanding of the Civil War. We made it a caricature of itself. If racist politicians cast the war, unintentionally, as a symbol of the worst of Southern history, it was easy enough for my friends on the other side to agree.

For my own part, though, I really didn't think about the war for a while. First as a student and then a young journalist, I was almost wholly absorbed in the present. My infatuation with the civil rights movement soon reached an intensity that was evangelical. And when I did return to the past, reconsidering the history that I had been taught, it was not the Civil War that caught my attention. Not at first. Rather, it was the brief but excruciating era of Reconstruction—a time my own grandfather remembered with such extraordinary bitterness.

He shared the prevailing Southern view that newly freed slaves, wholly unprepared for citizenship, surged en masse into the post-war vacuum to make a mockery of Southern politics. For white Southerners, the sudden presence of black officeholders was a painful symbol of Southern defeat, enforced by the presence of federal troops. In this telling of the story, there was precious little mention of the remarkable example set by some of these former slaves. In Alabama, for example, a freedman named Benjamin Turner—who had taught himself to read as a slave and had managed his owner's Selma hotel during four years of war—ran first for the Selma city council and then for a seat in the U.S. Congress. He won that seat in 1870, campaigning on a platform of "universal suffrage, universal amnesty." By that, he meant that former slaves should be allowed to vote, entering the mainstream of citizenship with a full recognition of their humanity. But he also campaigned for amnesty—for the notion that white Southerners who fought for the

Confederacy should not be punished for that decision.

" . . . Let the past be forgotten," Turner declared, "and let us all, from every sun and every clime, of every hue and every shade, go to work peacefully to build up the shattered temples of this great and glorious Republic."

In his pleas for unity and forgiveness, Turner joined other African American voices in the Congress—Representative Robert Smalls of South Carolina, Senator Hiram Revels of Mississippi—in an eloquent echo of Abraham Lincoln. "With malice toward none" resonated powerfully in their hearts, but that was not a part of my family's understanding. Not, at least, until the civil rights years.

That eventual change of perception is a reminder, I think, of the truth of William Faulkner's observation: "The past is never dead. It's not even past." And because it lives, it requires—cries out for—a periodic breath of new perspective. Thus once again, on the 150th anniversary of the struggle, my own generation returns to the story of the Civil War. We know the shame of the South's racial history, and know also that the war was fought—at least in part—in a gallant, desperate defense of that shame.

But we also know there was much more to it, more layers for the memory to engage; and perhaps it's possible after so many years—such a hard and majestic sweep of history—to grasp at a distance what some of the participants felt at the time. There was, absolutely, a heroism in this war, the kind that later generations remembered, and the generals, especially, would speak about the nobility of combat.

Thus did Robert E. Lee extoll, with a generosity and grace that define his memory, the "valor" of the men who served at his command. But there was also the cost in suffering and blood—as many as three million wounded and killed—and people North and South were stunned by the massive reality of loss. The letters of Franklin Gaillard drip with the horror of things that he saw, and the words of his father, as clearly now as they ever have, continue to echo down through the years:

Oh, this terrible war.

Throughout the letters written by his family, we can hear a hundred and fifty years later that fateful interplay of gallantry and pain, with the latter growing stronger as the war went on. And then came defeat. As this final reality settled hard on the South, there was no way to disguise it, no way to mitigate the despair. That task would fall to future generations. But at the time, there were many like my great-great-uncle, Richebourg Gaillard, who was twice taken prisoner during the war, and when it was over, returned to Alabama to try to pick up the pieces of his life. He found it hard, and in a letter to an uncle in South Carolina, written in 1866, he closed with this assessment of the future:

Of politics I will only say this; I see nothing ahead. All is dark and pretends no good for us of the south. The whole north is mad and nothing will cure their madness but bloodletting.

And there it was—not just a momentary depression, but a mindset filled with defeat and distrust, a bleakness that seemed to have no bottom. No wonder the sons and daughters of the next generation searched for consolation, some noble echo of the fierce Southern pride that helped bring the nation to war in the first place. No wonder the heart and psyche of the South—particularly the white South—became such a tangled knot. No wonder it has taken us all so long to remember with compassion those who lived and died in the war. They created, endured, the greatest tragedy in the tragic history of our land, but a moment in which, along with everything else, our better angels managed to survive. And our nation emerged not only intact, but with the promise of greater freedom still ahead.

Part II

Voices of War

The Letters

The Civil War letters excerpted in this section were written by Thomas Gaillard and two of his sons, Richebourg and Franklin Gaillard; two daughters, Lydia Gaillard Alderson and Marianne Gaillard Willison; a grandson, Thomas Palmer Gaillard; a cousin, W. P. DuBose; and an in-law, Augusta Evans Wilson. The voices do not speak as one. Franklin's especially is filled with Southern zeal—a dogged expectation that the cause of the Confederacy will prevail, even as he details the cost in blood on the battlefield. Richebourg moves from righteousness to gloom, while Thomas, the elder, who writes with a classical frame of reference, regards the war almost from the start as a tragedy of Greek or Shakespearean proportions. The other voices fall within that range, and the effect for me is a sadness that far outweighs Southern pride. Other readers may hear something else, for I have attempted in the pages that follow, with only the barest sketches of context, to let the voices speak for themselves.

Richebourg Gaillard, January 7, 1844

In this letter written to his uncle, John Palmer, Richebourg Gaillard gives voice to the kind of Southern defiance that would eventually lead to secession. In the excerpt here, written while he was a student at Yale College, Richebourg, in effect, apologizes for the earlier influence of his father, Thomas Gaillard, who had opposed the states' rights policies of U.S. Senator John C. Calhoun. The idealism of this letter stands in marked contrast to the resignation in those that Richebourg would write during and immediately after the war.

Dear uncle,

. . . In your letter you said you "hoped for the credit of the old South state" that I stood up bravely for southern principles and "for the Man and the Cause"—John C. Calhoun. In reply all I can say is that whenever the occasion renders it necessary that southern principles, the old south state and John C. Calhoun, should need a defender, I am always ready to exert my weak and humble powers in their defense. As far as I know myself politically there is no man living or who has ever lived whose ideas of government I can more thoroughly conform to than those of Mr. Calhoun. It was a long time before I could divest myself of the prejudices I had imbibed in youth against the doctrine of nullification which has "grown with my growth and strength." But in spite of the inclination given to my mind I have after an impartial investigation come to the conclusion that this is no consolidated government. The different states by the adoption of the Constitution did not become fused with one whole but rather in many respects still remained distinct and independent of each other, as they appear on the map, as with the stars and stripes on our nation's banner, that a great share of certain sovereignty over people by the states has never been parted with, that in cases not provided for by the Constitution they will be in their sovereign capacity the ultimate, supreme, and effectual law within their own territorial limits, in dependence upon other states and on the general government which is the mere creature of the states having its powers all distinctly defined by the Constitution—the instrument of agreement between the states and by which no power is given to the general government to decide in cases where the government and a state are the parties. In short, I am a states rights man . . .

FRANKLIN GAILLARD, APRIL 25, 1861

This is one of many letters Franklin Gaillard wrote to his sister-in-law, Maria Porcher, who assumed care of Franklin's children, David and Ria, after the death of his wife, Catherine Cordes Porcher. This was Franklin's farewell on the day he left South Carolina for the war in Virginia.

Dear Maria,

Our company or a large portion of them came over from Morris Island on yesterday. This evening about 11 o'clock we leave for Virginia. I was anxious to get off and go up and stay with you until the 1 o'clock train. But I can not do so. Can you not bring the children down and return on the 5 o'clock train this evening? I would like to see them once more and give them one last kiss. We are in for twelve months service. I am determined that so far as my feeble exertions are concerned our country shall be free of the despotism which these Northern people now hang over our devoted heads—if I survive the struggle I can again resume my labors and support my children—if I die—then I trust a merciful God and a grateful people will care for them. With love to all and many kisses I remain yours affectionately,

THOMAS GAILLARD, MAY 24, 1861

In this letter to his brother-in-law, John Palmer, immediately after the beginning of the war, Thomas Gaillard touches upon his diminishing health at the age of seventy-one, his difficulty in repaying a loan and continuing dependence upon his slaves, even though he has moved from his Monroe County plantation to the city of Mobile, and his fatalism about the war. From the vantage point of later generations, it is striking how little Thomas—from all accounts one of the gentlest, most reflective members of his family—agonized over the question of slavery. He apparently was one of many slave owners pushed, ironically, into righteous rationalization by the condemnations coming from the North. As his wife, Marianne, put it in an earlier letter to John Palmer, "God knows we are not the devils the abolitionists make us out to be." Thus did Thomas, who had once argued passionately against disunion, accept the inevitability of war against an enemy he thought could never be appeased.

Dear John,

Your letter of the 20th April was received in due time and you may think it very strange that I have not sooner replied to it. Your letter found me prostrated from a bowel complaint from which I have not entirely recovered. This has been a prevalent disease in our city but very few instances were fatal. There are few cases now existing, and with a few more days of warm and genial weather I trust the disease will entirely disappear . . .

But the more immediate object in view in now writing you is to reply to your request of a remittance. Had it been in power I would have felt it my duty to have done this long ago . . . I have negroes working in the city, and I depend wholly upon their wages for the daily support of my family. The proceeds from their labor have become so diminished, under the general embarrassment and stagnation in business that they fall short of my needs. Their wages are brought in weekly and I find at the close of the week I have not a dollar in the house to add to the proceeds of the succeeding week so that it is literally with me from hand to mouth. . . . What the issue out of our difficulties will be no human foresight can indicate . . .

This will be a sanguinary and merciless war. The south must do battle not only for their civil and political rights but for their property, their lives, and their domestic households. The invasion is one of the Goths and Vandals and they should be met in no compromising spirit.

Augusta Evans Wilson, late spring, 1861

A noted Southern author and in-law of the Gaillard family, Augusta Evans Wilson was an ardent advocate of secession who supported and modeled the strongest possible role for women in pursuit of the Confederate cause. Among other things, she nursed the sick and wounded from the Southern army, published a defiant, pro-secession novel called Macaria, *and on at least one occasion, traveled to Virginia on the eve of battle to offer her personal support for the troops. On a trip to the Hampton Roads Waterway in the spring of 1861, her party drew artillery fire from the Union garrison at Fort Monroe. In a letter to her friend Rachel Lyons Heustis, Wilson offered this account:*

While I was looking at its savage portholes the immense Rifle Cannon at the Rip-Raps thundered angrily, and to our amazement, a heavy shell exploded a few yards from us. I turned my glass at once on the Rip-Raps, and distinctly saw the muzzle of the villainous gun pointed at our party; saw the gunmen at work reloading, and while I watched a second flash sent its missile of death right at us. When a third ball whizzed over our heads and exploded in a field just beyond us, the officers insisted we should get out of sight, as they were very evidently firing at us, and our lives were in danger. Oh! I longed for a secession flag to shake defiantly in their teeth at every fire; and my fingers fairly itched to touch off a red hot ball in answer to their chivalric civilities . . . but nobody was hurt, thank God.

FRANKLIN GAILLARD, AUGUST 4, 1861

This letter from Franklin Gaillard to his father, Thomas, after the First Battle of Bull Run, or Manassas, was one of the first in which Franklin described, in poignant and vivid detail, the rigors of battle. It also reflected his early optimism about the course of the war.

Dear Father,

I have been wishing to write to you for some time, but everything has been involved in uncertainty and the duties of an advanced post were so arduous that I was resting whenever I could get time. Our lips were closed too by special order from Beauregard who forbid any communication, either private or public, revealing any of the movements of his army. I write occasionally to the *South Carolinian* and as that paper is sent to you I knew you were thus kept informed of my movements. At Fairfax we had a very trying time. Our Regiment is the first in the first brigade commanded by Gen. Bonham. We were therefore in advance, one company from this Regiment, and towards the last, two, being thrown out on picket duty so far in advance that we could hear the drums of the enemy and occasionally would see their videttes, or advanced pickets. When out on such duty orders were rigid not to sleep at night or throw off any accoutrements. Each company or companies would be on duty twenty-four hours. In addition to this there was guard duty, both in camp and village and also duty in the entrenchments. Our works were very extensive, though not very heavy. For three weeks before the advance of the enemy Gen. Beauregard had issued orders that our position should be abandoned rather than make a stand there against heavy odds. Our retreat was conducted in the most orderly manner, notwithstanding the advance column of the enemy was at times within half a mile of us and could have damaged us with artillery. But they were thrown off by our repeated stands as though we intended to give them fight. At Centreville we held over from two o'clock P.M. until 12 o'clock at night. Here we had a pretty strong position. The enemy formed in line of battle intending to attack us early in the morning but we gave them the slip and drew him on to Bull Run. At Centreville there is a very high hill upon which we were located. From this point to Manassas, Gen Beauregard's headquarters, telegraphic communication was sent during the day by means of a blue flag and at night by a turpentine ball lighted at the end of a long pole. They would make full strokes and half strokes to the right and left and then forward. By these signs long orders were communicated and intelligence conveyed in return. The history of next day's proceedings show how the enemy rushed upon us and were repulsed—how they renewed their efforts on Sunday and were routed. For upwards of seven hours our Regiment was on the march. About 12 o'clock we were ordered from the centre to the left. We marched about three miles to get to the scene of action. From then until near 8:30 o'clock at night, when we returned from the pursuit towards Centreville and lay down on the grass for the night at the Stone Bridge, was about seven or eight hours. A large number of the Regiment who had not been wounded gave out from exhaustion and were left in our rear. You can form no idea of the thirst created by the excitement and fatigue of battle. The indifference with which one regards the dead and wounded is another astonishing feature. After action when the enemy had been driven off I began to gather the canteens of the enemy for our own famishing men who could not leave ranks. The first I got containing water was on a dead man. The side of the canteen was bathed in blood up to the very mouth of the canteen on one side. My thirst was so great that regardless of this I turned it so the water would run out at the bloodless side, emptied it into my own and drank it. Before I went into battle the very sight of the blood of a dead man would have caused me to shudder. After our own men had been provided for I gave water to several of the wounded enemy. They seemed very grateful and were surprised at our kindness—it was so different from what their lying generals had represented to them. The battle sounded terrible but the destruction of life was not nearly so great as would have been supposed from the sound. The moral effect of the victory can not well be calculated. It has thrown confusion into the ranks of the enemy and in spite of the confident and defiant resolution of their Congress, has involved the whole object of the war in doubt and distrust. I feel very hopeful that next spring will end the contest and bring a recognition of our independence—it may come before that time. Our relations have been fortunate having gone through with only one of the party receiving a wound—this was Moultrie Dwight. A spent ball gave him a very severe blow on the thigh bruising and blackening it very much. We were under fire of a very heavy column—three or four times our number—our men having advanced to a fence by the side of which was a road that had worn itself down leaving a bank next to the fence that gave us protection. Moultrie was down on his belly with his gun through the fence, the butt at his shoulder and his right knee drawn up, while in this attitude and just as he had fired, a ball struck him on the thigh, passing very near to his head as you can perceive by imagining his attitude. We are here now at Vienna on the Alexandria, Loudoun and Hampshire Railroad. The cannons prepared for our reception in Washington we can distinctly hear. What our generals are going to do—whether take an advanced defensive position on the line of the Potomac or cross it and assume offensive operations remains to be seen. I wish I could hear something from you all. This is the third letter I have written since I came to Virginia in each I have begged to hear about all of you yet no letters have I received. I will close by giving you as good a draft of the battle field as I can. I forgot to say that a member of my company told me he saw Andrew at Manassas. He came on with an Alabama Regiment and was inquiring everywhere to see me. With love to all I remain

Your most affectionate son

FRANKLIN GAILLARD, OCTOBER 27, 1861

Two months after writing to his father, Franklin Gaillard wrote this letter to his young son David in South Carolina.

My dear Sonny:

Papa was very much pleased and very proud too, to receive a letter from his little son about whom he thinks so much. Papa never thinks of going into battle and being shot, but right off he thinks of his little David being left without him to impress upon him those principles which he would like to have govern and guide him when he grows to be a man. Little daughter will have an Aunt and a Grandma who will be sure to give her good advice and make a nice and useful lady of her. He wants his son to be always obedient and grateful to them too. He must be kind and polite to all, study hard at school, tell the truth always no matter what happens. He must make no friends with mean and untruthful boys, but associate only with those who are well behaved and honorable. He must be always brave too. Never do wrong—nor let others do wrong to him. That's the kind of a boy papa wishes his son to be. And then when he grows up to be a man, if war should come again and his country want his services he will make a good and faithful soldier. Papa hopes he will get through this war and live to set a good example to his son as well as give him advice—but if he should not, then he must remember all this and try to do as Papa would have liked him to do.

FRANKLIN GAILLARD, DECEMBER 31, 1861

As 1861 drew to a close, Franklin Gaillard was still optimistic about the war, even as he was beginning to feel its rigors.

Dear Maria

. . . We have been suffering a great deal out here from sickness. During the past week there were seventeen deaths in this Brigade. The winter has been mild so far, I suppose for this latitude. We have not had much rain, but some of our spells have been pretty sharp. We had weather about three weeks ago that froze pickles, pepper vinegar, etc. A piece of beef tongue was iced all through. Eggs were like a lump of ice. They could be cut through and neither the white nor yellow would run. We wash every morning now in iced water. The other night in riding from Centreville I had my moustache icicled. But still as we have had no snow and the roads are in good condition we are still agreeably surprised at weather so far. Before it sets in, in all its accustomed severity, I hope I may be able to go back to South Carolina and escape it.

You probably have seen the Act of the Confederate Congress granting furloughs to those soldiers who reenlist for the war or for two years. I am making efforts to reorganize a company and get a furlough for fifty days beginning about the latter part of January or first of February. The men are very much dissatisfied with Capt. Casson, through duplic-

ity and insincerity and other qualities, equally uncommendable, he has become very unpopular. I have such a contempt for his character that I would not take the 1st Lieutenancy much less a privates position under him. I never was more disappointed in any man. The consequence is that they have signified to me that they will not serve again under him—but seem disposed to volunteer under me. As I am determined to continue in service as long as the war lasts I should of course rather come back as a Captain than a private, and will use my efforts to reorganize it. Failing in this then I shall get a furlough on my own account. This will allow me to avoid the worst part of the winter, to go back and attend to business affairs and then to come back again—by the time the government will need my services. The Generals have refused to grant any more furloughs except to those who reenlist. This I think is right—for those who reenlist ought not to be refused, while those who will not reenlist expect to go home at the expiration of their time of service and should be held here as a reserve until we return … We are into the war fighting for all we hold dear and if we do not come up to our duty with a self-sacrificing spirit, we may lose all we fight for or at any rate allow the enemy to gain important advantages over us. I am sorry to say that all of our men do not take this view of the question and instead of doing all they can to meet the exigencies of the Government they construe the favor it shows the reenlisted men into an effort to force them. We are being pressed at all points and every Southern man must rally to his country's standard so that no advantage be gained over us at any point. I am sorry to think that our men in South Carolina are not as confident as they have reason to be. That they can whip the enemy I do not doubt; but I am afraid they do. If we maintain our position at all points I can not doubt that we shall have peace much sooner than many expect. It is utterly out of the question that any Government can prolong a war that costs them near two

millions a day. And if we nerve ourselves to do our whole duty without relaxation at any point the Yankees will cave in . . .

Tell David and Ria I hope I shall in the course of three or four weeks be able to give each of them a kiss. I have been keeping for David a bullet picked up in the battle of Manassas at the fence behind which our Regiment stood. I must try too and get up something for Daughter although she forgot to send something to Papa when the box came. With much love to all I remain

Thomas Gaillard, April, 1862

These are excerpts from a letter written by Thomas Gaillard to a now unknown member of the family in April, 1862, shortly after the Battle of Shiloh, the bloodiest of the war until that time. The entire letter was once in the possession of a Gaillard cousin, but has since disappeared. Nobody knows why Thomas's grandson, Samuel Palmer Gaillard, saved these particular paragraphs, keeping them in fact, until his own death at the age of 103. But they offer a poignant insight into Thomas's state of mind, as Southern fortunes turned dark and his sons and grandsons were still in the fight.

Oh this terrible war! Who can measure the troubles—the affliction—it has brought upon us all? It has pleased the Almighty to inflict upon us this severe chastisement—and it is our duty to submit in Christian spirit . . . We can not foresee His ultimate purpose in thus scourging our people with the direst of calamities. But even in the depth of our sorrow, we can also see a glimmering of mercy . . .

The contest is fast approaching a crisis, and I am not sorry for it. The sooner it is brought to an issue the better . . . Let His will be done.

RICHEBOURG GAILLARD, APRIL 20, 1862

This letter, written by Lieutenant Richebourg Gaillard to his brother, Dr. Edmund Gaillard, was dated simply, April 20, and mailed from Camp Chase, a federal prison near Columbus, Ohio, where Richebourg was taken after his capture at Island Number Ten on the Mississippi River. Terse and to the point, the letter reflects, once again, the increasing gloom among some members of the Gaillard family.

Dear Edmond

A Mrs Clarke who is permitted to visit the South via Norfolk proffers to take letters from the prisoners of this place to Richmond. By her I will send this. I wrote to my father a few days since, but for fear of a miscarriage, will write to you. Tom and Brutus have been separated from me. The officers were brought here and privates sent to Springfield or Chicago, Ill. I have written to both places to ascertain where our men are. Brutus was sick and in the hospital at the time of our surrender and I am not aware that he has as yet recovered. He had mumps. You all no doubt feel chagrined at the misfortune which has befallen the 1st Ala Regiment. We were taken without the firing of a gun. If we were sacrificed for the good of the Army at Corinth, all well; but if we were neglected by our superiors with no such purpose, then there is nothing to console us. We were 70 miles in advance of the line of operations in the Valley and our case a hopeless one after our communications on the river were cut off. When the first gunboat passed us we might then have retreated, leaving the sick and all munitions of war in the enemy's hands. Delay of 48 hours was fatal. We were surrendered eight hours before any of us knew it. How long we will be prisoners, God only knows. I am restricted. Remember me to all.

Franklin Gaillard, April 20, 1862

Still doggedly committed to his cause, Franklin Gaillard wrote this letter from a Confederate encampment near Yorktown. To his sister-in-law in South Carolina, he confided his shame that some of the men from their own state were growing weary of the fight.

Dear Maria:

Amid the excitement and suspense now involving us I will write you a few lines. A tedious journey to Richmond, a sojourn of several days there, a trip to Orange and back again to Richmond thence to this place via James River, a nomadic life since we have been here, bivouacking as best we could without tents, without even a tolerable supply of cooking utensils, and a necessarily limited supply of commissary stores gives a faint conception of what we have endured since we left Winnsboro. Here we are now face to face with McClellan's grand army, at this moment not more than seven or eight hundred yards from the enemy's line. As soon as we came down here we were put on picket duty with a small river flowing between ourselves and the enemy. Our pickets were shooting at each other continually, resulting in one fatal disaster to us. Lieut. McCain of the Camden Company went to the outposts and while indulging in the privilege of firing at the enemy was himself shot in the thigh by a minie ball. The bone was so much shattered and the muscles so much contused that amputation was necessary. The shock to his nervous system was however too great, and he died about thirty-six hours after. He leaves a wife and two children. Another of the thousands of sad sacrifices that have been made in the cause of our country's independence. God grant that they be not unpropitious. Two or three times we have been ordered out in expectation of a general engagement. Last night was one of intense anxiety. It was dark and rainy. Just such a night as the enemy may have chosen for an attack. There was more or less musketry and cannonading throughout. At 8, 10 and 1 o'clock, there were terrific volleys that roused us all up ready for orders. Our defensive line runs from the mouth of the Warwick River which empties into the James across the Peninsula to Yorktown. Near the source of the river dams have been constructed to back the water and increase the natural impediments. Along these dams which are above our present position there have been three or four very hot engagements. The enemy's design is to destroy these dams, bring their columns across and turn the fortified line between them and Yorktown. If the enemy attack us, which seems now almost certain, we shall have the most terrific battle ever fought upon this continent. The forces engaged will be larger than at Waterloo. I pray our cause may be favored with signal victory. Beauregard and Van Dorn have dealt staggering blows to the invader in the west. If we can route McClellan's boasted columns here, by vigorous prosecution, such as the Conscript Act of Congress promises, we may bring the war to a speedy termination. Thursday last we were all deeply mortified by the action of some of our troops. The period of enlistment of many of Regiments having expired, the War Department, very properly, under the emergency, ordered them down here; there was so much grumbling and dissatisfaction at being as some termed it "pressed" into service that Gen. Magruder issued an order to send to the rear out of harm's way all who were unwilling to stay. Would you believe it of South Carolinians that while the cannonading of the battle was sounding in our ears, telling us that the conflict had begun, near about four hundred gave up their arms and marched off! About half of them as the sound of battle grew louder overpowered by a sense of shame returned with deep contrition. The remainder so soon as Gen Magruder heard of the passage of the conscript act, were ordered back to their Regiments, unless pronounced physically disabled for service.

Near two hundred left Bacon's Regiment, about one hundred and thirty left William's, twenty-four from Cash's and upwards of thirty from our Regiment. Wyatt Aiken I am informed by gentlemen in Bacon's Regiment was very prominent as vindicator of these refugees from battle. He was so instrumental in the dissatisfaction that Col. Bacon came very near arresting him. This conduct here added to the disreputable behaviour of the troops of one of our Regiments in Augusta will very much sully the reputation of South Carolina.

Some of the men who returned said that they met two young Louisianans coming out of the fight, with their mouths blackened with the cartridges they had been biting, and having in charge a prisoner. These boys said appealingly to them "Men what are you doing without your arms? We want you all yonder in the fight." This was too much for them and they hurried back to their Regiments. Yet even this appeal many of them resisted. I am very glad the Conscription Act has passed. You will see it in the *Richmond Dispatch* which I subscribed for and sent to Mrs. Egleston. Do give my love to all at Clifton and many kisses to David and Ria. If I were better fixed I would try to write a longer and more interesting letter. Hoping that I may soon be able to write accounts of a great victory and of the safety of all of us I remain,

FRANKLIN GAILLARD, OCTOBER 14, 1862

This letter, written shortly after the bloody battle of Sharpsburg, still anticipates a Confederate victory, barring a defeat on the western front of Confederate armies under Generals Bragg and Van Dorn. Franklin also offers reasons why Gen. Robert E. Lee will not, as rumored, invade the North in the coming year. Franklin was wrong on all counts.

Dear Maria:

Your letter was received by me a few days ago. It had been some time that we had heard and its contents afforded me great pleasure. Indeed taking it altogether it was the most pleasing letter I believe I have received since I have been in the service. The good tidings of my relatives in Alabama, the return of Richebourg and the account of [Cousin] Brutus' vitality, the health of the family in Winnsboro . . . altogether made up an unusually satisfying bulletin. I was glad to learn too that my brief note from amidst the dead and dying of Sharpsburg battlefield had been received. When I wrote it the general expectation was that we would have another battle either that evening or the next day—the falling back of our army not being then a thing known. Several others sent letters off at the same time and all have since learned that they reached their destiny at a time of intense suspense and anxiety . . .

Our battles have come so often and so many have been killed that we have all got into the habit of associating the wish to live through with everything that is spoken of in connection with a return home. There is no doubt about the seriousness and truthfulness of the great uncertainty—but the wish is so common that it is becoming a joke. Our regiment, in fact the whole army, has increased very much in numbers. We have been encamped at this place since the 29th of September. During that time we have drilled a great deal. I have been strict with the Company Officers and have been drilling both the companies and battalions. As a reward for my efforts it is conceded by all that the Regiment is in better state of discipline and drill than it has ever been since in the service. Col. Kennedy came back yesterday and resumed command. His return imposes upon me the arduousness of nothing to do. So if we remain here much longer I shall begin to hunt up acquaintances in the neighborhood. I have generally managed to pass my time very pleasantly in this way. I have had several invitations from friends to go with them to Winchester and be introduced to families there, but being in command I preferred to remain with the Regiment. I think it time I was rewarding myself for dutifulness. Among the celebrities of Winchester is the famous Miss Belle Boyd. Persons who have seen her represent her as very fast and not among the most respectable people of the place. Capt. Wallace who has been going to church there every Sunday tells me that they have a very nice Episcopal Church, a good choir, and a fine organ. Such music will be a rare treat.

My impression is that we will not remain here much longer. I cannot understand why McClellan should be so quiet. It seems to be imperative upon him to do something and that very soon as the winter is nearly upon us. Possibly he is slow here because he intends to make Norfolk the base of operations for the winter. If so, then we shall have very soon to move down from here. I have little doubt that he will make another desperate effort to take Richmond. If then he is whipped we may consider the war practically ended. Unless while we gain advantages here Bragg or Van Dorn should lose in the West. Every northern paper tells us that their credit is tottering and decaying every day. Another defeat of their grand army will paralyze them. I think the people of the South should be prepared for reverses during the winter: They must be met with unfailing hearts. Then as Spring breaks in upon us we must break upon them with our whole force. This will give us peace. Practically the war will, in my judgment, end next summer and peace come upon us sometime during the winter or Spring ensuing. I am sorry some of our cracked brained editors had induced you all to hope so much from invasion of the north. To invade the north, now after two years of war, would require an army and preparations and expenditures which would have taxed us severely at the beginning of the war when we were fresh and vigorous and our credit at its prime. This is going to be a war of financial exhaustion and we should conduct it so as to involve the north in the heaviest expenditures while we husband our resources. This we can best do by defensive war. It is simply ridiculous to talk of invading with such an army of stragglers as we have and straggling can not be avoided unless the Government has it in its power to put its Quartermaster, Commissary and Medical Department in better condition. This it can not do, cut off as it is from the world and with undeveloped manufacturing resources. Our people must be courageous and enduring and not lose their patience in hunting out short plans of ending the war. If it lasts no longer than three years we may consider that we have won our independence in a short time when we consider the power and numbers of our adversary. You know I never underrated them and when the revolution began went into it with the expectation of a desperate struggle. I was surprised at their being so dispirited by the defeat at Manassas and began to hope that one more general battle in which I of course expected to whip them would end the war. But they have recovered from that and no people could be more firm and unshaken in their purpose than they are now. Nothing is going to stop them but the exhaustion of their strength.

I am afraid I am going to suffer this winter. I have neither a blanket or woolen clothing of any kind. I am anxious to get me a pair of boots . . .

RICHEBOURG GAILLARD, DECEMBER 16, 1862

Richebourg Gaillard wrote this letter to his brother Edmund, following Richebourg's exchange as a prisoner of war and his return to active duty at Port Hudson, Louisiana, on the Mississippi River. The letter was written at a time when the Union army and navy were converging on the Mississippi, seeking to split the Confederacy in half. Richebourg describes his unit's shelling of the Essex, *a Union ironclad, and of another wooden boat nearby. He also offers thanks for supplies and clothing sent by Southern women to the troops at Port Hudson. Such civilian support of Confederate soldiers was a common practice during the war, and many of the Gaillard women took part.*

Dear Edmund

The things you sent by Tom Roach and Mr. Miller were duly received. Be so kind as to return our thanks to the ladies who were so kind as to remember us in their labors to alleviate the necessities of the soldiers . . .

We have nothing of interest here except the little cannon fight which occurred about four miles below and in sight of us yesterday morning. Some three days ago the Essex and two armed wooden steam boats schooner rigged anchored below our batteries and out of reach. One of the wooden boats left the next day. The Essex and the other remained until on yesterday morning, and left under these circumstances. Night before last Capt. Boone with three of his field pieces supported by two companies from our Regt. under command of their respective captains, Isbell, of Talladega, and Williams of Barbour, crossed the river and under cover of the night posted the pieces behind the levee and about 400 yds from the boats. At day-light they opened on them and a brief cannonading was kept up for about ¾ of an hour. Our gunners, it is said fired very accurately and succeeded in hitting the wooden craft at least 50 times out of 75 shots. Our men say they could distinctly hear the cries of pain from the wounded on board. Suffice to say that the Essex was soon put in motion and went off down the river towing her consort. From this fact it is inferred that her machinery was injured. This argues well for this post. About the 20th of Sept. when the Essex ran the gauntlet from Vicksburg she is said to have been pierced by several shots from these batteries here, and now we believe we have crippled another. There were no shots fired at the Essex yesterday. As she is a huge ironclad it was deemed unnecessary to try to injure her with light guns.

I must close here. Remember me kindly to your wife and to the little fellows.

THOMAS PALMER GAILLARD, DECEMBER 16, 1862

Thomas Palmer Gaillard, son of Edmund, was stationed with his Uncle Richebourg at Port Hudson, and penned this note to the bottom of Richebourg's above. Soon afterward, Tom Palmer, as he was known in the family, was killed by a Union sniper. He was still a teenager when he died.

Dear Father

As I have not time to write you a letter, I thought I would add a few lines to Uncle R's. Return my sincere thanks to all who were so kind as to send me things. They all suited me splendidly excepting the pants that Mr. Matthews sent, they were both too large. By altering them though I can make them do. I have enough clothes now to do me for a long time to come . . . with the exception of a jacket or coat, which ever is the most convenient for you . . . Let me assure you therefore that I have not grown an inch since I left, so when you send things again to me remember to cut them by my old ones. Give my love to Mother, and children, and kiss them for me.

FRANKLIN GAILLARD, APRIL 5, 1863

Franklin Gaillard, having been wounded at the Battle of Fredericksburg in December, 1862, wrote this letter to his sister-in-law, Maria Porcher, shortly before returning to action in the Battle of Chancellorsville.

Dear Maria:

. . . We began to anticipate very early activity here. With a bright sky and high wind the ground and roads had dried wonderfully. Last night a little after dark it began to snow and continued unceasingly the whole night. This morning the ground was covered to the depth of six or seven inches. The wind was blowing very high and cold as it has been for two or three days. It is still cloudy, and cold with every prospect of more snow during the night. I regret it only on account of our horses. The men are all very comfortably fixed in huts, or what must be called so, for the language has no word for the nondescript concerns they now inhabit. Our animals suffer terribly—exposed to these cold winds with no food but corn many of them have died. Among the number I am sorry to place my Malvern Hill mare. Her gentleness, intelligence and quickness and love of motion had attached me very strongly to her. Her death touched my pocket even stronger than it did my heart. For as she was the only one I had I have had to buy another for which I have had to pay five hundred dollars. Living not far from our camp is a Mr. Alsop—a very wealthy, intelligent and reliable gentleman from Fredericksburg. As soon as I conversed with him I recognized him as a gentleman upon whom I could rely. You have no idea of the prices asked and the jockeying carried on in horses. Besides picking up an animal at hazard without knowing with whom you are dealing, even if by chance it happens to be sound, you have no guarantee that he has not been stolen and that he may not be claimed. So as this one suited me in size and action I determined to give the high price for her. Her grey color is an objection but one of secondary importance. My only objection to the snow is that it endangers the existence of stock so precious. That it keeps the Yankees back I rejoice. I would like for the roads to continue impassable so that they may make their effort at Charleston before they advance here. Our government can thus use the forces in North Carolina at either or both points if necessary. I think we have men enough to repel an attack upon our front here. I am not so confident if a flank movement is made. It might necessitate our falling back nearer to Richmond, obstructing and delaying the enemy's movement until we are stronger. I believe we could whip them with the number now present in a fair open fight, but could not make it as decisive as if we had fifteen or twenty thousand more. These we could get if they are whipped off from Charleston or if they can be delayed until it becomes too sickly for them to operate by land down there. I have been all anxiety to see the result of the contest for our City. I have very strong faith that they are going to be most ignominiously driven back. The attack of their iron clads upon Fort McAllister has inspired me with great confidence. I do not think their boats or the men in them will be able to stand the terrible concussion of heavy metal that will be thundered upon them from our forts and batteries. We are surely so well fortified by land as to be able to whip them ten to one there and it is out of the question that they can bring such odds. I am more anxious about Vicksburg than any other point. I received a letter from my nephew Tom of the 42nd Ala a few days since. He says the "Yanks will never be able to open the Mississippi River for the Northwestern people." I received a letter from Father today. He tells me he has heard from my brother Richebourg and my nephews, Palmer and Brutus of the 1st Ala. Reg. since the fight at Port Hudson at which they are stationed. They were well and untouched during the engagement. My brother Sam and Tom he says are now at Yazoo City. They are in Moore's Brigade, Maury's Division. From the manner in which they are being moved about I think the intention is to put them in the first fight that occurs there . . .

Father mentions in the letter which I received from him today that he wrote me a letter in January, directed it to Winnsboro and that he enclosed in it $100.00 which he intended as a present for David & Ria. I suppose the letter is lost. But if it should turn up in Winnsboro open it and take it out and dispose of it for them as you think best.

One advantage gained by buying my horse is that I have formed the acquaintance of the ladies of Mr. Alsop's family and have spent two or three very pleasant evenings with them. Their daughter, Miss Nannie, is a very sweet, accomplished young lady. Mrs. Alsop is a genuine old Virginia lady. She gave me an Enfield rifle which was left by a Yankee in her house in Fredericksburg. . . .

With kisses to David & Ria and love to all in Winnsboro and at Clifton, I remain yours affectionately

FRANKLIN GAILLARD, JUNE 11, 1863

Having survived the Battle of Chancellorsville, a Confederate victory, Franklin Gaillard wrote this letter as the Confederate army under Gen. Lee prepared to move north toward its fateful encounter at Gettysburg. After musing about the general fortunes of war, and about mutual acquaintances, Franklin offered a post script about rumors of an upcoming march.

Dear Maria:

I received yesterday the package about which you spoke in your last letter. I assure you there was no necessity for the apologies you and Mrs. Egleston make for the shirts. They look very neatly and if they will only wash well they will serve my purposes as well as the finest quality. Tell Mary I am very much obliged to her for the envelopes. They came in very opportunely. Tell Daughter the soap is very nice. I put it to immediate use to get rid of the dust of the march. The roads are excessively dusty from the prolonged dry spell we have been having here. Day before yesterday the cavalry had us out in line of battle to resist a reconnaissance in force which the enemy made on that day. We suffered very much from the sun and dust. Our nights are quite cool however, and two blankets to cover with are not uncomfortable. Ever since my first entrance to the service I have been particular about sleeping warm and comfortable. No fatigue on the march or prospect of a fight ever induced me to throw away all my bed clothes. I attribute my health in a great measure to this. For several days before I left Fredericksburg I was feeling quite unwell and had a slight fever for several days. I began to think that I was getting typhoid fever. I am just now recovering from a cold. It is singular that I should have passed through the severity of winter without being once indisposed from this cause and should be affected now when summer is upon us.

I miss my friends of Fredericksburg very much. The evening I left Moultrie and went to an ice cream and strawberry entertainment at the Misses French. They are sisters of Mrs. Alsop. We met the latter and Miss Nannie there and spent a very pleasant evening. We had a regular supper table bountifully supplied and about an hour or so after we went into the supper room again and had ice cream, strawberries, frozen something else that was very nice, cakes etc. We remained there until after 11 o'clock and then set out to overtake the Brigade—after a ride of seven or eight miles we came upon them encamped near Chancellorsville. Those people back there are in great trouble about the Yankees coming in upon them. It seems to me if I were so situated I would move off entirely out of reach. Mr. Alsop is a very large property holder and has suffered severely in negroes and in damage to his real estate. The place he is living on near where we were encamped was very much damaged by our own troops clearing away and burning his woods and destroying enclosures. He has another place below Fredericksburg on the river. This the Yankees occupied when they crossed over the second time and threw up entrenchments upon it and

tore down all of the buildings upon it. They also have a fine residence
in the town which through the kindness of Mrs. Alsop I occupied for
a week … She went in and carried bed clothes and fixed me off very
comfortably. I found the same destruction here. The Yankees both times
that they occupied the town made it a hospital for their wounded. The
bookcases, sideboards, wardrobes, chairs, chandeliers, in fact everything
were broken up in the most wanton manner. To add still more to her
troubles some fifteen or twenty Yankees were buried in her gardens. Our
own people had dug an entrenchment through her flower garden. As she
takes great pride in housekeeping and in her gardens you may imagine
how much it must distress her to visit the town. Besides all this four or
five cannon balls had been shot through the house.

     We had quite a fight here day before yesterday among the cavalry.
The Yankees crossed over at two or three points and surprised our men
at every point. I hear the conduct of the 2nd S.C. Cavalry and 4th Virginia Cavalry very severely commented on. The Yankees charged these
two Regiments and broke the first who gave away and ran headlong
back upon the Virginia Regiment which gave away also and the Yankees
chased them like rabbits taking a number of horses and several men. The
impression at first prevailed that they had suffered severely but their men
came in afterwards. Frank Hampton the Lieut. Col. was killed and Col.
Butler lost a leg. Hampton was the only man killed in the Regiment. On
the left toward Brandy's Station on the Railroad the fighting was more
creditable. The 1st S.C. Cavalry did very handsomely. The fight lasted all
day but as usual with Cavalry they charged and counter charged doing
very little damage to each other. Here we took some four or five hundred
prisoners and four, five or six pieces of artillery. The Yankees managed
to get completely in rear of Gen. Stuart and cut off for a while his communication with Gen. Lee. The whole affair was more like a sham battle

and has rendered cavalry in my opinion more contemptible than ever when it comes to services upon the field of battle. If I were in that service I would quit it. I could not stand the contemptuous jeers the infantry give them when they come about. I have not been able to hear anything from the 6th S.C. Reg. for some time. I hear it rumored that they are at Hanover Junction but can not get positive information. I wrote to John Bratton just after the battle of Chancellorsville—but have heard nothing from him. He opened a correspondence with some spirit and I was in hopes he was going to keep it up.

Lieut. Col. Goodwyn of this Reg. came out and spent two or three weeks with us. He found that he could not stand the service and has resigned and gone home. This will promote me one grade and make Capt. Wallace Major. As soon as notification of the acceptance of his resignation is returned from the War Department the order for our promotion will be published. I have been called Major so long I have a friendly, familiar regard for the title.

I was very much shocked to learn the death of Miss Bessie Bacot. How revolting death is when it visits one so· young and interesting. It is really a melancholy occurrence. I received a letter from Lydia and another from Father a short time since. They are both well but have no news from the boys at either Port Hudson or Vicksburg. I have been and am still exceedingly solicitous concerning these two points.

Kiss David and Ria for me and give my love to all at your Mother's and at Aunt Louisa's and remember me affectionately to Cousins Sallie and Sarah and the girls at John Bratton's and believe me,

Yours affectionately,

I do not know where we are bound for yet but still think a forward movement is designed.

FRANKLIN GAILLARD, JUNE 28, 1863

This was Franklin's last letter before the Battle of Gettysburg, written to his son, David.

My dear Sonny:

I promised in my last letter to Aunt Ria that I would soon answer your letter. We have been so constantly on the move then that I really have not been able to do it satisfactorily. When I received your letter we had just begun our move. I had no idea that it was the beginning of so grand a movement as it has resulted in, here we are now in the great and powerful State of Pennsylvania marching forward in the direction of her Capitol. I do not know, of course, what Gen. Lee is going to do, for like a good general he will keep his intentions to himself and his Lieut. Generals. But it appears to me very much as if he is going to strike a blow at Harrisburg and if he can succeed in taking it, it will be a brilliant triumph of our arms. The enemy have nothing but raw troops in our front. I think we can whip these three or four to one. Then we could march on towards Philadelphia and Gen. Hooker would have to come to our front to save it and we would thus free Maryland and maybe take Washington and Baltimore. Thus summer is going to be filled with great events and if Providence will favor our efforts I hope mighty things for our country will be achieved. Our Army never was in better health and spirits. Since we left Fredericksburg we have marched about one hundred and sixty miles. In our march from Culpepper to Ashby's Gap we had a terrible march. The sun was very hot and then so many men marching along together made it very dusty. Another thing too, in the old settled country the farmers find great difficulty in getting rails. Where we passed it was mountainous and stony and the people would gather up large quantities and make stone walls which answer the purpose of a fence and are very durable. When our troops would be down in a valley, so that no wind could refresh them, with the sun coming down heavily upon their heads, the heat increased by the reflection from the walls, and the dust stifling them so that they could not breathe in pure air, the gallant fellows, many, very many, would turn red in the face from blood rushing to their head and fall to the ground with sun stroke. When we got to Ashby's Gap we stopped two or three days and then we had a very heavy rain and one or two days of cloudy and wet weather. This revived them all like pouring water on wilted plants. Nearly all came up. We stopped there to guard this Gap and it was well we did for the enemy's cavalry assisted by a small force of infantry drove our cavalry several miles before them and we all thought whipped them pretty badly. We had crossed the Shenandoah River and had to recross it and go back three or four miles to keep the Yankees from taking the Gap. Next day the Yankees went back and Stuart's cavalry went poking along at a very slow pace is if they were in no great hurry to overtake them. They now claim in the papers that they drove them back but we who were there and saw them know better. Our cavalry is very little account and have very little to boast of. There are more than half of them who are with their horses lamed or sore backed with the wagons. I am glad to see that the newspapers are speaking very severely about them and I hope it will improve them. They have got so now that as soon as a fight begins they think they have nothing to do but to go to the rear and let the Infantry do the fighting. Our boys ridicule them very much whenever they pass.

I am afraid our men will suffer for shoes. These long marches are very trying on men's feet and shoes. You would be very much amused to see the men crossing a river. A regiment is marched down to the banks and sometimes halted long enough to allow them to pull off their pantaloons. If the water is over waist deep they put their bayonets on their guns and hang their cartridge boxes on them—then right shoulder shift arms and wade across all in fine spirits as if it was a frolic. The Yankees carry pontoon trains along with them but our boys say that every man in General Lee's Army carries his own pontoons. It is very funny to pass through these Yankee towns to see the long sour faces the people put on. The girls, some of them, wear little United States flags. Others more indecent hold their noses and make faces. Our men go on and pay no attention to them. They only laugh at them when they make themselves ridiculous. Things are very cheap here in their stores but they will not take our money and Gen. Lee has issued very stringent orders about private property. He is very right for our Army would soon become demoralized if they were allowed to do as many of them would like to. Many of them think it very hard that they should not be allowed to treat them as their soldiers treated our people. But we must not imitate the Yankees in their mean acts.

We are getting a large number of horses but this is being done by proper authorities. Gen. Lee is going to support his Army over here and this will tax the people here and make them feel the war.

You must give my love to all and kiss daughter for me. Give my love to Grand Ma, Aunt Ria and all at Aunt Louisa's. It is getting so dark I can hardly see how to write.

FRANKLIN GAILLARD, JULY 17, 1863

This is Franklin's first surviving letter after the Battle of Gettysburg. In it, he reports on the condition of friends and family involved in the fight, inquires about relatives and friends back in South Carolina, and gives a candid and vivid account, at times horrifying, of Confederate casualties in the bloodiest battle of the war. He also seeks to convince his sister-in-law, or perhaps himself, that the war even now can still be won.

Dear Maria:

I received your letter of the 24th day before yesterday. I have been intending to write to you for some time. But we were so continually on the move and the wagons with writing material not being convenient I have delayed longer than I should have done and longer than I would had not Moultrie and Bosie both written to relieve the anxiety of home folks. Another terrible battle has been fought and I am yet safe. Moultrie too passed through untouched. Poor Eddie received a very painful wound and one which will give him trouble for some time. I stopped at the Brigade Infirmary as we were retiring from Gettysburg and saw him. He was suffering a good deal of pain and seemed to dislike very much being left in hands of the enemy. I regard his wound as severe but not serious. There will be published in the papers a list of casualties. I took a great deal of care in the preparation. The reports of captains of companies were submitted to the surgeon to obtain concurrence of opinion as to the nature and extent of wounds. The battle of Gettysburg was, I think, the most sanguinary of the war and was as clear a defeat as our army ever met with. Our Brigade suffered very severely. The 2nd Regiment I have no hesitation in saying was the hero Regiment of the Brigade on the occasion. I can not recur, even in thought, to their gallantry without the proudest emotions. We received orders to advance. As soon as we started we came under fire of the enemy's batteries. For four hundred yards our line moved beautifully forward not wavering nor hesitating in the slightest degree. We were to take a battery immediately in our front. I never saw men more resolved upon an accomplishment. We had crossed two fences and our line was unbroken although many gaps had been in the ranks. In the midst of this beautiful advance the regiment to our right commenced moving by the right flank, that is, by facing to the right. The directions we received required us to dress to the right so that this regiment would face to the right and then to the front. We would have to conform supposing that the orders came from Gen. Kershaw. I afterwards learned that it did not. The consequences were fatal. We were, in ten minutes or less time, terribly butchered. A body of infantry to our left opened on us; and as a volley of grape would strike our line, I saw half a dozen at a time knocked up and flung to the ground like trifles. In about that short space of time we had about half of our men killed or wounded. It was the most shocking battle I have ever witnessed. There were familiar forms and faces with parts of their heads shot away, legs shattered, arms torn off, etc. Yet moving to the right but not retiring we occupied a piece of woods which gave us protection until the battery was taken by the Mississippi Brigade under Gen. Barksdale. The Regiment of our own Brigade to our right fell back before a very heavy body of infantry. Notwithstanding all this, our men stood their ground. The enemy's infantry came up and we stood within thirty steps of each other. They loaded and fired deliberately. I never saw more stubbornness. It was so desperate I took two shots with my pistol at men scarcely thirty steps from me. I could not see that I did any damage but there were some seven or eight dead lying just about where I was shooting. Wofford's Georgia Brigade coming up on our left supporting the Mississippi Brigade, we charged upon the party opposed to us and drove them pell-mell through the woods, shooting them down and taking prisoners at every step. We pursued them to the foot of the stone mountain, the strongpoint in their position, where we attacked them. Here the bullets literally came down upon us as thick as hailstones. It is scarcely necessary to say we fell back. But the Yankees did not venture to pursue. We held until next evening the larger portion of the battlefield we fought on. It was thickly strewn with their dead.

The battle was an unfortunate one. Our army went into it in magnificent style and I never saw it fight better but the position defeated us. For this I blame our Generals. In a day by our injudicious attack they defeated the most brilliant prospects we have ever had. It was caused by their overconfidence. The greatest misfortune is that it destroyed the unbounded confidence reposed in Gen. Lee. Before, the army believed he could not err. They now see that he can once in a while. Viewed in a political aspect, it was a disaster to us, in my judgment. Its injurious effect can only be counteracted by them attacking us and being well whipped. I think such will be the result. I hope they may come dashing upon us, expecting to find us demoralized. Our men suffered terribly for shoes. Our ammunition became short and our line of communication was so long that we lost a great many wagons. I am more satisfied than ever that invasion is too hazardous for us.

The fall of Vicksburg I take quite patiently. I made up my mind when Fort Donaldson fell that the Mississippi River was gone. I do not believe they are going to gain one tenth the advantages from it they anticipate. Had we not invaded Pennsylvania we would have been in a condition to reinforce the armies in the West. We will have to fall back and give the enemy deeper lines to operate through. Gen. Bragg has almost checkmated Rosencrantz by this policy. I feel very anxious to hear from my brothers and nephews.

I regret that the Yankees have got a footing on Morris Island. I think we should still act in the defensive. Let them charge our works. I see some of the papers are urging Gen. Beauregard to give them the bayonet. Fools! they forget that the slaughter at Fort Wagner was owing to the enemy attempting to give our men the bayonet behind their works. An unsuccessful attempt to storm the enemy's works would involve terrible loss of life and probably seal the fate of Charleston. It may fall anyhow. But why accumulate disaster? They cannot sap and mine on the Island. It is too wet and sandy. Let them dig their parallels. They will have finally to storm our works. Then will be our opportunity. God grant that Charleston may not fall but if it does I hope our men will not be penned and captured so that we will have nothing left to keep the enemy from advancing. Any place can be taken with men sufficient concentrated and to spare.

Capt. Wallace, now Major, and Col. Kennedy were both wounded and have gone home on a sixty days' furlough. Adjutant Sill was also wounded and has gone home on a forty days' furlough. Mr. Boozer the Colonel's orderly who messed with us lost a leg and was severely wounded in the arm. He was left in the hands of the enemy. So that of the five in the mess I am the only one left. Lieut. Perry of Co H and myself are the only two of the old officers of the Regiment left with it. Lieut. Pelot of Sumter is now acting as my adjutant. I have him messing with me. I feel quite lonely at times, but my increased responsibility diverts me, as only one of the old company commanders is with his company. The others are all inexperienced and slow to assume authority. So that I have some trouble on this score.

When I commenced this letter we were at Bunker Hill between Winchester and Martinsburg. I was prevented from finishing it. Put it in my trunk and have not been able to conclude it until now the 27th of July near Culpeper.

Our army is all here recruiting rapidly and will give Mr. Meade a warm reception should he come down upon which I am disposed to doubt.

In the package of things sent home by Moultrie there is a pair of shoes, a present to Daughter from Gen. Kershaw. I got nothing in Pennsylvania or Maryland in the way of clothing or goods of any kind. The people did not want to trade and our money was really worth little or nothing to them. There was an immense amount of plundering. Our army would have been demoralized had we been victorious and remained long over there. Now that we have got back to Virginia it is very hard to break the men from their acquired habits over there. The people looked at us with sour faces, long faces, and indifferent faces. All they seemed to fear was that we would burn their houses. Horses and cattle they gave up as small matter.

Tell David and Daughter I did not get one thing for them or for myself. I hope I will soon get another little letter from David. Now that Daughter has gone to school I suppose she will soon be writing letters too. I enclose the order promoting me to the rank of Lieut. Colonel. Tell David I make him a present of it. I am glad to hear of Allee's promotion to Captaincy. Give my love to all at your Mother's, Clifton, and John Bratton's. I am sorry Betty had so short a visit. Tell her when she writes to do me the favor of abusing John for me for not writing. He began a correspondence in fine style and in the same fine style dropped it after enticing me into two or three long letters. I have not heard anything definite of Jenkins Brigade for sometime.

Bosie and Moultrie are both well. Remember me to Cousin Sally's family and Mr. Robertson's.

FRANKLIN GAILLARD, AUGUST 12, 1863

In this letter from the summer of 1863, Franklin Gaillard, still the family firebrand, sought to rally the spirits of his family at home, in the wake of Confederate losses at Gettysburg, Vicksburg, and Port Hudson. He praises the stubborn leadership of his own army's generals, and clearly shares—implicitly, defiantly—the South's final hope that the North will ultimately grow weary of the contest. Union casualties, after all, had been as staggering as those inflicted on the South.

Dear Maria:

I received your letter day before yesterday, I was glad to hear that you have all escaped sickness. I hope your fear of a sickly summer may not be realized. There is certainly enough trouble, disease, and death from war in the land to exempt us from those arising from pestilence. From the tenor of your letter I am afraid you are all too desponding. That we have received staggering blows there is no disguising. But they are such that we can recover from, for the enemy suffered severely in inflicting them. Both at Gettysburg and Vicksburg they paid heavily for whatever they achieved. What pains me more is to see the improvidence of our journals in attacking our Government and our Generals. They do it in such a way as, if believed, to undermine all confidence in them. In such a struggle confidence is indispensable to success. How can our people be expected to make the heavy sacrifices now required of them if they believe that imbecility presides at Richmond and madness governs at our Army Headquarters? Every man feels that he is paying a prodigious price—his life at stake, his property in the balance—the prospect of success is all that gives him strength for the exigency. It is expecting too much of human nature to suppose that intelligent people (who know that, in an unequal contest such as this, physical weakness can only be remedied by superior wisdom and skill) can contend in hope and confidence if they are convinced that this superiority is woefully wanting. The editorials of the Sentinel please me immeasurably. I wish the paper was taken by every family in the Confederacy. I hope you get it regularly.

The fall of Vicksburg has been relieved of much of its severity by the favorable terms which Pemberton succeeded in making. You remember when Fort Donaldson fell I gave up the whole Mississippi. Our Generals astonished me by holding out longer than I thought they could. They are doing only now what I thought they would have to do then—fall back and concentrate. You see how Gen. Bragg has held Gen. Rosencrantz in check by falling back when he could not cope with him on advantageous terms. Gen. Johnston discomfited Grant in the same way by falling back from Jackson. Our people must become reconciled to this thing of giving up territory and cities when concentration for strength requires it. They must at any rate not become disheartened by it. Whenever the enemy presses upon us after his ranks have been filled by a grand recruiting spasm we can only parry the heavy blow he would then deal us by falling back and forcing him to take up deep lines of communication—so that we can play in his rear with our cavalry and force him to detach large portions of his force to protect his line. When we have by falling back spun out his force sufficiently we can then turn upon him and drive him back. I am not at all discouraged by the operations of the Summer. The capture of cities along our coast or rivers does not discourage me—however much I may regret it. That can be accomplished by perseverance and engineering. I have not the slightest fear that the Yankees will ever be able to bring out as large a force against us as we have already whipped.

I have not heard one word directly from my family in Ala. since the fall of Vicksburg and Port Hudson. I have written twice to Father but received no answer. Your letter informing me of poor Tom's death was the first news I had from that quarter.

We are all here quietly enjoying our rest. Our Regiment is steadily recruiting from its severe trials. I am getting on pretty smoothly now. I had to exercise some severity when I first took command. I came down tightly on officers and by punishing three or four of them I soon got everything I wanted.

I hope Aunt Louisa may be restored and your Mother benefited by their trip to the Springs. Tell Liz I wish I was with her to assist her in entertaining her company and keeping an orderly house.

With many kisses to David & Ria and love to all the family,

I remain yours affectionately

Do excuse this miserable ink, paper and pen and consequently writing. I enclose $100 which you can use as your judgment suggests.

FRANKLIN GAILLARD, SEPTEMBER 6, 1863

In this excerpt from a letter to his sister-in-law, Maria, Franklin again voices his displeasure at Southern newspapers criticizing the Confederate government and the leadership of President Jefferson Davis. He expresses the hope that women on the home front will continue to shore up public support for a war that remains in his mind a struggle for Southern independence and freedom.

Dear Maria

. . . I do not blame papers for finding fault with the Governments for no Government is perfect and I think it proper that a newspaper indicate when errors have been committed. But to uproot all basis of confidence in the public mind is mischievous in the extreme. I do not see how any paper having the good of the Cause purely at heart can continue in a course calculated to destroy confidence in the Government after the developments in North Carolina have demonstrated its evil tendency. The *Mercury* and *Standard* are working together in getting up a tone of absolute distrust. When they accomplished this they would diverge very widely—the *Standard* would say then reconstruct, the *Mercury* would say revolutionize, subvert the present Government and put Mr. Rhett or

Mr. Toombs at the head. With a faction then for a regular Government and another for the revolutionary Government—the two papers would again come together in the result they would accomplish—viz: Yankee supremacy.

The Army and the Government must work together harmoniously to achieve success and these must be sustained by a wholesome dispassionate and confident public sentiment. The Army here I know is right—for a home sentiment I look to the women of the country in the main, and to the old men. The large class who have been sheltering themselves behind exemptions laws and substitutes are utterly incapable of appreciating the exultation of independence or the degradation of subjugation.

I have at last heard from my brothers and nephews in the West. Sam and Tom came safely through the Seige of Vicksburg. Tom Palmer, my brother Edmund's son, was killed at Port Hudson from his own indiscretion. He would climb upon the fortification to see what the Yankees were doing though continually warned against it. In one of these daring observations he was shot in the head. Richebourg is again a prisoner. He was at last accounts at New Orleans. I enclose a letter from him to Father. Brutus Howard had to walk 200 miles after he was paroled before he reached Mobile.

Father and Lydia are ready at any moment to leave Mobile. Sister and Nan and Peter's wife had already cleared themselves and taken refuge in the country . . .

FRANKLIN GAILLARD, OCTOBER 5, 1863

This letter was written after the bloody battle of Chickamauga, a Confederate victory achieved at great cost. Even for Franklin, the strain of war was beginning to show.

Dear Maria:

I have delayed, an unusually long time after our recent battle, writing to you. I have never had such a reaction as followed our recent trials and hardships. From the time that we broke up camp in old Virginia extending several days after the battle of Chickamauga we were tumbled about night and day until we were almost worn out. When the terrible excitement of battle was over it took me a week or more to recover from the depression of reaction. We are still living very roughly. We did not get our tent until day before yesterday. Until then we were taking refuge under such shelter as we could construct from our scanty supply of blankets and India rubber clothes. Very fortunately I swung a country-made coverlid and a rubber cloth across my shoulder so that whenever we camped for the night I had something to secure for me a comfortable rest. All of the field officers of the Brigade were without horses, so we had to foot it. The night before the battle we marched nearly the whole night. Next day about 11 o'clock we were put in the fight, though we were marched out and kept some two or three hours in reserve awaiting the time when we should be ordered in. It is a period of great suspense as you may well conceive. As we were advancing we met one of the Brigades of the Western Army, McNair's, coming out full tilt. We expected every moment that the advancing columns or lines of the enemy would soon be in sight. What they were running from I could never learn. We were being constantly informed that the western Yankee was a very different animal from the eastern—considerably more of a tiger and altogether terrible. The western troops were particularly anxious to impress this upon us and could we have been whipped without imperiling the fate of the battle I believe most of them would have been pleased. We were moving in to the support of Hood and we needed nothing but our eyes to tell us that our comrades of the Virginia Army were sweeping along like a tornado. Every now and then we would hear the old battle yell, while captured artillery and prisoners were being carried by us in a continued stream. Finally their force was expended and as our Brigade emerged into an open field our advance having hitherto been through woods, we found that the enemy's right had been so pressed back that our line of battle was perpendicular to his front. We immediately changed our direction to the right so as to meet him. He had formed his line upon the brow of a high ridge called Peavine Ridge, his right resting in the woods. To the rear of his line and extending two hundred yards was a gentle rise intersected with ravines, and culminating at the summit ridge. The whole was covered with a growth of heavy oak timber and very little underbrush. This line on the brow they had guarded, not only with infantry but with eight pieces of artillery. From this position Hood's men were recoiling after having expended their force in splendid advance. As we would pass the wounded of this Division they would say "Press them, boys, press them, they will give as quickly as the Yankees in Virginia." As we were changing front to meet them they seemed to think we were wavering and hesitating to attack them so they waved their flags defiantly at us. Our line being established we began our advance. My Regiment was on the left of the line and I was directed to advance so as to break their right resting in the woods. The whole line then moved on in splendid style, not faltering a minute and with not much loss drove them from their position and took every piece of artillery they had. We followed up and met their second line at the summit ridge strongly posted. As we approached this we were met by a very destructive fire. The right and center of the Brigade suffered severely, so much so they were ordered to fall back to the position their first line had held. This left our lines still very near to each other. As yet my command had suffered but little. After we had fallen back my right companies suffered severely. A Brigade was then advanced upon our left but did not go much in advance of us before it fell to the ground and began to fire furiously from that position. The enemy then encouraged raised a shout along their line and began to advance. The Brigade to our left belonging to the Army of Tennessee, broke back in a run. This of course threatened to leave our left flank unprotected. The old 2nd stood like a rock. They called this Brigade to stand fast and cheered so as to encourage them. Our example and encouragements had the desired effect and they rallied promptly. The Yankees advanced but we drove them back very quickly. In ten minutes we had them retiring. Seeing their confusion, I ordered the 2nd Regiment to charge them. We again advanced and took possession of the hill in our front but being unsupported either on my right or left, I reluctantly had to retire my line to its original position. General Kershaw remarked to me that so gallant a charge ought to have been more successful. We lost a good many men in this encounter. About an hour later another advance was ordered and that Brigade on our left and the 2nd Regiment were ordered to advance. 'Twas not long before that Brigade again left me and I remained under fire until sunset. By that time we had lost a number of men. I saw shot down around me some of the finest men of the Regiment. Lieut. Brown of Company A was killed at this time. I regretted his death deeply. There never was a truer and braver spirit. There is something peculiarly sad in the death of a young foreigner like him, who not simply from a spirit of adventure but from a noble inspiration to defend and maintain the right—espoused our cause. He has never heard one word from any of his family and he often told me that they no doubt thought he was fighting in an unrighteous cause but he said they thought so because they were ignorant of the true state of affairs. 'Twas he that called out to the companies on the left to cheer and rally that Brigade as it was passing on. Whichever of his old comrades survive the war I hope they will see that proper respect is shown his remains. I shall most certainly make it my duty should I be one of the survivors. Twenty-one more of our gallant band have given their lives to the cause and soon we will be called upon to make another offering. At this rate who of us can expect to pass through except the maimed and the crippled? The 2nd Regiment—heroes of a dozen battles—passed through Charleston under the most trying circumstances, after having been absent more than two years and bound direct for another great battlefield and people hardly turned their heads to look at us. . . . It is rumored now that we are to be sent to Mobile to meet Grant's Army. If we have a fair opportunity we will whip him too. We all begin to feel that the Southern Confederacy is on our shoulders. These troops here do not fight for victories. They do not know how to fight Yankees. From what I have seen of them, I am not at all astonished at the failure of our Army in the West.

Tell Daughter I received her original letter and prize it very highly. I will answer it soon . . .

We seem to have come to a halt here in sight of Chattanooga. I went up on the Lookout Mountain the other day and enjoyed very much the magnificent scenery. It is said that five states can be seen from it. The interest of the natural scenery is very much enhanced by the view of the two armies spread out before you. It is rarely that such a sight is enjoyed.

Give my love to all at Aunt Louisa's and Cousin Sally's. With a kiss to David and Ria and love to all, I remain

Yours affectionately,

FRANKLIN GAILLARD, NOVEMBER 10, 1863

Writing again from east Tennessee, Franklin recounts his happiness and surprise at a chance meeting with his brother, Sam Gaillard, who brought with him news of other members of the family. He writes dispassionately about his "servant," Henry, who has accompanied him to war, and about the inconvenience of Confederate officers having to feed the slaves they have brought with them into the conflict. Regarding the war itself, he speaks philosophically about the possibility—even the probability—that he might be wounded, as he was at Fredericksburg the previous year. He mentions again his distaste for war, but seems to harbor little doubt that God is on the side of the Confederacy.

Dear Maria:

As we are quietly fixed today near the little village of Sweetwater in East Tennessee I design a letter to you. Your last letter relieved me very much as I was worried at my remittances to South Carolina being lost. The expenses of the service are increasing so rapidly that I would have felt the loss of that amount severely. Since coming out here I have had to buy another horse. Nina having become so lame I was forced to leave her in the hand of a Quartermaster in Petersburg. I never saw the man before and know nothing concerning him. If he is an honest man I will recover her. If not, I will lose her. In these days of general rascality and speculation the chances I acknowledge are against me. If I lose I shall be somewhat consoled by the reflection that it was a matter of necessity, not of judgment. My present steed, Fanny, as Henry, my servant has named her, is serviceable but not so fine an animal as Nina. I got her for $400.00 quite reasonable considering the prices prevailing.

The bag of flour you sent in to Bosie and myself came in good time and was highly acceptable. Since we have been in the service our fare has never been so bad as while we were around Chattanooga. Five days out of the seven we drew a pound and a quarter of corn, ground, husk and all—'twas just like dog bread when baked, and a pound of beef. The other two days we drew a pound of flour and a third of a pound of bacon. An officer can draw rations, although he pays for them, for only one servant—as Colonel Kennedy had three and Maj. Wallace two we had more mouths than we could supply fully . . .

On my way from Chattanooga to Tynah Station on the Railroad from Chattanooga to Cleveland I met some Vicksburg troops. I was advancing to ask them what Brigade or Regiment they belonged to thinking I might learn something of Sam and Tom when I met right face to face with Sam who was hunting for me. The meeting you may know was no less pleasant than surprising. He was going one way and I another so we could not be together more than half an hour. It was a great disappointment to have to part with him so soon. I had not met him before for ten years. He was going to the same place along the line that we had left so that I would have seen a great deal of him had we remained near Old Lookout Mountain. Tom had stopped to see his mother and family so that I did not see him. Sam had been home but a short time before he left for the Army. He left them all well. He is heartily sick of the war. He is the most domestic member of the family. Never troubled himself much about public matters and could always find enough to engage him at home. His children he says can not understand why he does not remain with them and that seems to worry him. Father has not yet left Mobile and thinks now there is no immediate danger of an attack there . . .

We closed our campaign last winter with a successful encounter with Burnside at Fredericksburg. I hope we may repeat the achievement in the finality of this. If the parallel is carried out it will be my time for getting a momento of the affair. I hope it may be no more serious than those given me at Fredericksburg. I can hardly hope to get through safe in another battle . . .

Such is war. Providence seems to demand these sacrifices to warn us of the inestimable boon for which we contend. War is a terrible alternative and I shall always be proud of the fact that our country exhausted every effort to avoid it. We only chose it in preference to degradation. More sacrifice will doubtless be demanded of us. We can only pray God to stay the further exaction of blood but if he exacts still more before he grants us that for which we struggle, patience and acquiescence in his demand and hopefulness of final success must be our supports. Failure would be to us universal death.

Franklin Gaillard, December 18, 1863

As winter brought a reprieve from the fighting, Franklin found time to write to David back home in South Carolina.

My dear Son:

Five or six weeks ago I wrote a long letter to Daughter and told her I would soon write to you. But we have been kept so busy since then that I could not fill my promise. We have been shut up in these mountains so that it was very seldom we could get letters off, we have been in great suspense to hear from home. You, I know, have all been anxious to hear from us. I am glad that I can now write and say that we are all well. We have had an extremely hard time. Our communication being almost entirely cut off we have had to depend upon the country for all of our supplies. If you could see all the men and all the horses we have in the Army you would wonder how it was possible to feed them without railroads or steamboats to bring things to us. We have more men than there are people in the whole of Fairfield Dist. and more horses than there are in three or four Districts for there are seven or eight thousand cavalry along with us. Then there are our wagon horses and artillery horses. How we will manage through the winter I can not see, unless we go back towards the Railroad at Bristol in South Western Virginia. You can find that on the map. Bean's Station from which I am now writing is not on the Railroad but is an old trading station when this country was occupied by the Indians. We had gone to within seven miles of Rogersville when Gen. Longstreet turned back and came to this place to try and to capture some Yankees here. Our cavalry went in their rear and we attacked them in front. But their infantry came up in rear of our cavalry and made them get away. We attacked them here and took a large number of wagons and horses. The cavalry took a great many too. So that altogether we got from them more than a hundred wagons. The 2nd Regt. and the 8th of this Brigade attacked them and drove them from their position. In my Regt. three men were killed and about twenty wounded. Uncle Bosie had one of the best men in his company killed. He was one of the purest Christians in the Regt. His name was Richard Newmann from Columbia. Since we left Chattanooga I have been in four or five skirmishes and have been kindly protected from all harm. Col. Kennedy was again wounded at Knoxville so that I am again commanding the Regiment. We have been in so many battles and seen so much hardship that it is now quite small. It makes me feel sad when I remember how many brave and noble men have been killed or died who were with us at first.

With all of our troubles we manage to have a good deal of spirit sometimes. There are more rabbits here than I ever saw before in any section of the country. We go out hunting them sometimes and have very exciting scenes. About one hundred men on foot and fifteen or twenty on horse back form in a long line across a field and then march forward.

All are armed with sticks and as soon as a rabbit jumps up they run at him whooping and yelling and throwing with their sticks. If he escapes and outruns them, which rarely happens, then the horsemen give chase and run him down. A few days ago we went out, Gen. McLaws and Gen. Kershaw forming part of the cavalry's force, and caught upwards of sixty. That beats your hunts does it not?

The weather is very cold now and the wind is blowing quite keen. Here we are sitting around our camp fires with the smoke constantly blowing in our faces and the white flaky ashes covering our clothes and annoying us in many inconceivable ways. Christmas too is near at hand and we shall not be able to get home to enjoy it around a comfortable fireside with our own people. How much we would all give could we fly away and drop down unexpectedly among you. The war I am afraid has impoverished Old St. Nick so much that he will have to hide his head in sorrow and pay no happy visits to the little ones of our suffering country. Never mind, a bright day will yet come and the old fellow will be as merry in the South as he ever was. I sent back, in the tin box sent out to Uncle Bosie, an old coat and old pair of pants. The old coat I wished to have turned wrong side out. I want the collar and cuffs plain, without any of that blue cloth. I also sent an old pair of pants which I do not know what to do with. If it can not be made into something for you, it might make a vest for me. There was also a piece of calico, six yds. which I bought when in Virginia expecting to have it made into two shirts. But we moved off and I could not have it attended to. As I have never seen any ladies or women in this country who looked as if they could make a decent shirt I sent it back to South Carolina. Give my love to all at Clifton and at your Grandma's and kiss Daughter for me. Be a good boy and study hard.

Your affectionate father

FRANKLIN GAILLARD, FEBRUARY 27, 1864

In this letter to his sister, Lydia, Franklin writes sadly and wistfully about the death of his father, Thomas Gaillard, whom he had not seen in more than a decade. There seems to be a trace of ambivalence about Thomas's lack of success as a planter, which often forced him to borrow money from relatives, but a deep respect for Thomas's Christian philosophy and character.

Dear Lyd:

For two or three days past I have been most anxiously looking for a letter from some of you. Two days ago I received a letter from Maria Porcher enclosing one from Peter to Aunt Louisa conveying the sad news of the death of our dear Father. I can not say that I was surprised. The letter he wrote to me while I was in Winnsboro was so expressive of infirmity and decay that I was deeply moved by it and regretted then and still more now that I had not obtained before I left Camp permission long enough to enable me to go on to Mobile. It is a melancholy reflection to me that while he has only been dead a few weeks I have not seen him since 1853. Since then what changes have taken place. How many near and dear have been numbered with the dead. We may almost say that the preponderance of our affections are with the grave. Tattie (Franklin's wife), brother, mother, Sister Catherine, Willisson, Alderson, Tom Palmer, Father and in Fairfield David, Uncle David, Mattie, Willie and Eddie. The number is startling. Father's death does not strike me with the same poignancy that it does you who will miss him socially. To me the privilege of his society has long been lost. I can therefore view it now as you will after some time has elapsed. He was spared to a good old age. I remember hearing him say more than once that he had no desire to live after the infirmities of age should have impaired body and mind and brought on dotage. 'Tis true his mind was as yet unimpaired, but

I have seen clearly through his letters that his strength was failing him and particularly did I see this in his last. Who can say under the trials of this terrible war how long it would have been before he would have been reduced to the condition he so much dreaded? Who can say amid the trials that may await us as a people a just God in consideration of the upright and holy life he has led may not in mercy have removed him where in peace and glory he may enjoy the angelic communion of those who have preceded him. Father's life has been an illustrious example to all his descendants and I trust in God it may have its influence even to generations of our family yet unborn. The veneration in which I have always held his character has nerved me in many a moment of temptation. I am satisfied that there is no being living who can point to anything mean or little in his character or disposition. His rule of action was so near that of the Christian Philosopher as humanity could practice it. His want of success in worldly matters I attribute solely to this source. His letters and mother's I have tried to preserve—the former for the calm and noble sentiments of philosophy which pervade them—the latter for their sentiments of ardent piety and devoted affection. We may all cherish with pride the recollection of such parents. What an achievement it would be for their children could we all live as they did and die with the same hope of blessed immortality. How often when my soul seems moved by some agency to aspiration for its purchased heritage has it gone back years and years to the old family circle and pictured a praying father kneeling by the old red covered family Bible and a responsive mother joining heart and soul in his earnest implorations. Such scenes of devotion are never lost. They may pass unheeded for years—perhaps for a life time—but there are moments, I believe, in every one's life, when they will come back and speak to the very inmost soul and move and soften even the sternest nature.

I am very anxious about you all. From last accounts the enemy seems to have designs upon Mobile. Where are you going to and what arrangements you will make I should like very much to know. I see that Gov. Watts and Gen. Forney have been using all their efforts to get the people to leave the city. Write soon and let me know. I am very anxious also to hear all the particulars of Father's death, and send me too any obituary notice that may be written and let me know by whom it was written.

Give my love to all. Maria Porcher announced all well in Winnsboro in her letter to me.

I remain your affectionate brother,

Lydia Gaillard Alderson, late spring 1864

Franklin Gaillard's sister, Lydia, penned this brief epitaph to the bottom of the letter just above, noting with no embellishment Franklin's fate in battle some two months after the letter was written.

Last letter received from my dear brother who was killed at the battle of Wilderness.

Marianne Gaillard Willison, late spring 1864

In another marginal notation on the same letter, Franklin's sister, Marianne, was slightly more expansive—and more philosophical.

Poor Frank was killed at the battle of the Wilderness in Va. a few weeks after writing this. He little thought then that his brave and noble spirit would soon join those who had gone before. Such is life. What is it compared with eternity?

Franklin Gaillard, February 29, 1864

Franklin Gaillard wrote several letters about the death of his father. This one, written two days after the letter to his sister, was his reply to Maria, his sister-in-law, who had given him the news.

Dear Maria:

I received your letter three days ago enclosing one from Peter to Aunt Louisa announcing the death of my Father. It was the first intelligence I received of it. It saddened but it did not surprise me. I noticed particularly in his last letter very painful symptoms of decay-so much so that I regretted exceedingly that I had not more time that I might pay him a visit. I have been desirous for years of going to Alabama on a visit and I kept hoping each year that the next would find me with time and means sufficient to do so with ease and take Ria and David with me. But for this war I would long before this been able to spare both. Could I have anticipated this event I would have gone even at the expense of my pride in borrowing money. It has been eleven years since I was in Alabama. Great changes have taken place since. Then I was with Tattie; and Father, Mother, Brother John, Willisson, Sister Catherine and Tom Palmer were all alive.

To me Father has long been lost socially except through the medium of letters. I can therefore view his death as it affects himself and in doing so I do it with less of that horror of death that most persons entertain. I do not know whether the familiarity with death here in the service or the frequency of its visitation to the circle of those near and dear to me or both combined have produced a stupid and irrational insensibility to it; or whether the process of reasoning, through which my mind and feeling have been tutored in reconciling myself to its afflictions, is gone through with more rapidly from being so frequently practiced of

late years—probably both insensibility and rationality have had their
influence upon me— it is yet certain that I do not regard the removal of
those near and dear to me with the same poignancy of grief that I once
did. In viewing Father's death then, as it affects himself I can not grieve
heavily over it. As you say in your letter he had lived more than his al-
lotted time to man. In April he would have been seventy-four years of
age. The last thirty years of his life was devoted to such studies as weaned
him from this world and prepared him for another. He was as thorough a
philosopher as I ever knew. Reverses of fortune in his business relations
that would have distressed others were turned undisturbingly from him
by the stern Christian philosophy in which he had tutored himself. I
have never in my life known a person who believed and practiced more
consistently the doctrine that whatever happens is for the best and is so
ordained by God. The same philosophy I will guarantee fortified him in
death and that with this faith he met the Monarch with as little fear as
ever a mortal did. His Christianity steadied and tempered him in every
circumstance and relation of life. It gave to his character a consistency
that was complete. He was fully prepared for death. I have often heard
him say that he had no desire to live until the infirmities of age had impaired his mind and body. I have heard him cite with admiration for his
judgment and resolution the conduct of the Hon. Nathaniel Macon who
fixed upon seventy as the age which he would retire from public life, and
resolutely at that period went back to private life. He contended that no
man's faculties could be relied upon with certainty after that time. That
was my Father's belief and when I saw such unmistakable signs of old age
in his last letter and of which he himself was aware I know he met death
with no reluctance. Who can say under the trials of this terrible war so
exhausting to the nerves of the old how long it would have been before
he would have been reduced to the condition he so much dreaded? As

it is he lived just as long as he could enjoy life and died just when in all probability it would have begun to be a burden to him. Who that knew him can help from feeling that, in consideration of the pure and upright life he had led, a merciful Providence has removed him from trials to which the stoutest of us are but barely equal. His life has been an illustrious example to all his descendants and I trust it may have its influence upon generations yet to come. The reverence in which I have held his character has sustained me in many a temptation and impelled me in the right course. I am sure that no person living can point to anything mean or little in his character or disposition. The memory of my Father and my Mother I shall ever cherish with pride as well as veneration; of Father for the pure and exalted sentiments of Christian philosophy which guided him calmly and serenely through life, and of Mother for the ardent piety and devoted affection that peculiarly distinguished her. How often when I have been softened by affliction has my mind gone back to nestle in the old family circle with my Father kneeling by the old red covered family bible and my Mother responding with all the fervor of her heart and soul to his earnest supplications to the throne of God. Such scenes are never lost however much they may be neglected.

I have no news to communicate. Our Army has fallen back to this place on account of the loss of our cavalry, the greater part of which has been ordered to the West. Bosie I am in hope will get his furlough in a few days. Give my love to all at Aunt Louisa's and your Mother's. Kiss David and Ria for me.

FRANKLIN GAILLARD, MARCH 18, 1864

Franklin Gaillard was killed six weeks after writing this letter to his son, David. It was one of his last letters home.

My dear Sonny:

I received your letter the other day while we were on the march from Greeneville to this point. I was very glad to hear from you and to see how much you were improving in writing. I feel quite proud of all the letters I get from you and Daughter. You must write often and every letter you write will improve you and cause you to write with more ease. You must tell me about everything. How your pony is getting on and when you last saw him. Every little thing you tell about your Grandma's and Aunt Louisa's place will be very interesting to me.

I am very sorry that I never carried you and Daughter to see Grandpa Gaillard. You would both have loved him very much. Nothing delighted him more than to amuse and entertain his grandchildren. It is a great disappointment to me that you never saw him and knew him so that as you grew up you would study and conduct yourself so as to be worthy of such a Grandfather. I have kept a great many of his letters and your Grandma Gaillard's and when you get older they will be interesting to you and Daughter.

I have been very anxious to hear some particulars of his death. Up to this time I have heard nothing besides the news I got through Aunt Ria's letter. I think some of them must have written but if so I have failed to get the letters.

We came from Greeneville down here to meet the Yankees who were reported to be advancing upon us. They are still in our front but show as yet no disposition to come any farther on. Gen. Longstreet has gone to Richmond. I think as soon as he returns he will advance upon them.

He is not in the habit of standing off and looking at them long. So that I would not be surprised if we had a battle in a few days. I am now in command of the Brigade and would feel quite proud to command it in battle. While we were up at Greeneville we had a review of the whole of McLaws' Division commanded by Gen. Kershaw. Gen. Buckner was out to see the review. I commanded the Brigade. There were a large number of ladies out to witness it. I intended when the review was over to go and gallant some of them home—but Fanny spoilt all my anticipated pleasure by getting lame, very unaccountably, upon the field. I afterwards had a drill of the Brigade which Gen. Kershaw and several other officers and ladies witnessed. Gen. Kershaw told me he wished me to drill before Gen. Buckner so that I gave them a drill three hours long. You may imagine how tired they were. I wish you all could have seen the Division review. The line was as long as from Grandma's to Mr. Robertson's. When the General had ridden down the front and around the rear of the line, all then marched by him in companies in line. Every Brigade had a band of music playing in its front. After the Infantry had all passed then came by a battalion of artillery. The people about Greeneville who are friendly to the South were delighted with the display of so large a number of troops. The mean Tories did not like it much.

Tell Uncle Bosie not to forget to look for the brass hook for my sword about which I told him. Tell him I was very sorry he was not elected Lieutenant in his company. If his friends had all been present he would have got it. He must not resign the Sergeancy in his company. He must hold on to that so that he will not give offence to the members of his company.

Give my love to all at your Grandma's and Aunt Louisa's. Tell Daughter that little walk being finished I am looking for a letter from her. Tell her I send her the sweetest kiss I have.

Your affectionate Father

W. P. DuBose, June 17, 1864

A little more than a month after the Battle of the Wilderness, Franklin Gaillard's cousin, W. P. DuBose, who served as chaplain of Franklin's brigade, and later as Dean of Theology at the University of the South in Sewanee, Tennessee, wrote this letter to Maria Porcher, to be shared with other members of the family.

My dear Cousin Maria:

I have been waiting in vain for a period of rest in order that I might write to you at some length the circumstances of Frank's death but this painful campaign gives no indication of a speedy termination and although we are more unpleasantly situated than usual for writing, I will delay no longer. I know what an affliction Frank's death would be to you and to all who knew him well, and if I had had anything very definite to communicate beyond the few facts which I wrote home and which I knew you would hear I would have written to you immediately. What his loss is to us of the brigade as an officer and as a man it is impossible to overestimate. It would gratify his friends to see how deep and universal the feeling has been and how irreparable his loss is regarded. But there is a deeper source of anxiety which I know absorbs your interest as it has done mine and that is the consideration of Frank's spiritual condition and preparation for the great change which came to him so suddenly.

I have felt deeply on the subject. I do not think that any death outside of my immediate family has ever affected me more deeply. I had become more and more attached to him and took the sincerest interest and pleasure in the very evident growth and gradual deepening of his religious impressions. Of this I had no doubt. He was for some time with us in command of the brigade and I observed a growing undercurrent of seriousness and thoughtfulness which was perceptible to me even when a less interested observer would have been seen only an air of superficial carelessness. On Sundays he would read his Bible for hours, evidently with the deepest thoughtfulness and reflection. I seldom while we were in East Tennessee went to his tent on Sunday that I did not find him engaged in this way and he was regular in these exercises on other days. I observed him closely without appearing to do so. We frequently spoke indirectly on the subject but I hesitated to appeal to him directly or to attempt to draw from him a confession of the true state of his feelings.

I thought and still believe that I could effect more by getting gradually into his sympathy and confidence than by producing a restraint between us by intruding too soon into his inner and most sacred experiences. You can probably sympathize with me in the difficulty of approaching men of his class and character on this most delicate of all subjects. It is one of the problems of my professional life how to do this without doing more harm than good. When we came to Virginia and there was a probability of our soon meeting the enemy, I determined to make this my excuse for a candid talk with him on the subject . . . The very next day we started for the Wilderness and barely got there in time to save the day. The night before the battle the 2nd Regiment was separated from the brigade and I had service with the latter and talked with a number of the men. But all the time Colonel Gaillard was upon my mind and as soon as I could get off I went around to his tent hoping still to have an opportunity of talking with him. We had been marching very hard until after dark and I found him in bed with several other officers and asleep. We resumed the march at 1:00 A.M. and at sunrise became engaged with the enemy. As Frank was marching into battle I rode up to him and spoke to him. I told him that I trusted that his life would be spared, but above all, that he was prepared spiritually for anything that might happen. He shook my hand with evident feeling and we parted. An hour or two after I met him as he was brought out near the same spot, but he was no longer capable of talking. I have reproached myself bitterly for not having done more, and known more of his spiritual condition. I am convinced that if we knew all, there would be much to comfort us and alleviate our grief. That can not be now repaired. May God forgive me for what I failed to do in this as in all similar cases and give me the spirit and the ability to do better in the future. If he had lived I believe that the time was not far distant when he would have professed a faith which was beginning to show its fruits within him. It is a bitter disappointment that he was taken before our hopes had become assurance. Life is filled with these trials. Let us be grateful for the hope which we have and leave the rest with Him who alone knows the secrets of hearts. This uncertainty is painful but it is a blessing compared to hopelessness. God does not always admit us to the sweet blessing of absolute assurance . . .

Henry, I suppose, told you what disposition we made of Frank's property here. One horse for which he had not paid was taken by Major Wallace and the debt assumed by him. His riding horse Colonel Bratton has and will account for. I have taken his saddle at the uniform Gov't price (it was a captured saddle to which a fixed price is attached by Gov't—$50.00). This I will pay either in discharge of debts which he left here or to you.

Henry told you of his burial. I read a portion of the service over him and Dick carved a head board to mark his grave. I never performed a sadder duty.

May God bless you all and spare you further trials of this sort during this sad war.

Your affectionate cousin,

Richebourg Gaillard, September 9, 1866

Franklin Gaillard's brother, Richebourg, who survived multiple battles and the experience of being a prisoner of war, wrote this letter from Alabama to his uncle, John Palmer, in South Carolina, the state in which Richebourg was born and the place where many of his relatives still lived. Here, he gives a report on the Alabama branch of the family, including his brothers, Edmund and Sam; his sister-in-law, Caroline; and his nephew, Tom. He speaks somewhat caustically about the living, but fondly of the memory of another nephew, Tom Palmer Gaillard, and his brother, Franklin, both of whom were killed in the war. Finally, Richebourg offers his personal and gloomy assessment regarding the uncertain future of the South. Like many white Southerners, he was deeply cynical about Reconstruction politics and refused to play a role.

My dear uncle,

. . . Judging you by my own feelings I take it for granted that the first information you would desire would be of the family . . . Brother John's widow (Caroline Gaillard) with her children resides in Mobile. She has five single daughters, all of whom, with the exception of one or two, are marriageable . . . .

Tom, the oldest male member of (John's) family, who during the war was adjutant of the 42nd Alabama, is now connected with a counting house in Mobile. He is a good man who made for himself a fine reputation in the army. He is very popular wherever known and with the exception of a little inclination to tippling when amongst friends he is fair in every respect . . .

Of Edmund next. He belongs to that class who seem determined not to rally from the terrible adversities that have befallen the people of the south. His first wife died in 1861, and the following year he married a Miss Matthews, a young lady whose father before the abolition of slavery was regarded as one of the wealthiest men in our county. . . . His eldest son of two, Thomas Palmer (Gaillard), was killed during the siege of Port Hudson. Was a member of my company . . . I believe his death made a profound impression upon Edmund. He can never speak of him without shedding tears. He was, I will say, a noble boy . . . .

Sam was doing well before the war. Was making money. His property consisted mostly of slaves . . . He has a very industrious family.

Of myself I can say only this . . . I am entirely dependent on the law and under the law which is now in full force in this state the realization of the profits of my labor is postponed. I make enough to live on comfortably with the prospect of living something handsome within years. . . . I was offered with the promise of no opposition the position of delegate to the state convention last fall. I refused for reasons you can well conjecture. I was then tendered the nomination to the legislature and for the same reasons I refused that.

. . . Of politics I will say only this; I see nothing ahead. All is dark and pretends no good for us of the south. The whole north is mad and nothing will cure their madness but blood-letting.

Do pray Uncle John when you receive this sit down and write me a busy letter. I want to hear all about your good people of my mother state. I am yet devoted to her and her reputation and would like to know how you all are doing, what you suffered from the Yankee invasion and soldiery and hopes you have for the future.

I would like to hear of my brother Frank's children. I am devoted to his memory . . . As soon as I am able I shall make an effort to have his remains removed to South Carolina—the land he loved and for which he died.

SAMUEL PALMER GAILLARD, MARCH 26, 1956

At age one hundred, my grandfather, Samuel Palmer Gaillard, who was nine when the Civil War ended, published a small book about the Gaillard family in which he reflected on, among other things, the end of the war and the pain of post-war Reconstruction. It remained for other generations to wonder how those same years must have seemed to Southerners of a different background, particularly the newly freed slaves, who set out to assume their place as citizens, but found themselves soon stripped of the vote and shackled by segregation laws. The civil rights movement, which began before my grandfather died, forced many of us to reconsider not only the Southern present, but the past. Even so, there remains an authenticity in the anguish of my grandfather's memory. He was one of the last of a Southern generation who lived through the war and emerged from it scarred by bitterness and loss. His perspective began with older relatives' memories, which soon became seared into his own. His father, Samuel Septimus Gaillard, was a proud Southern man, an owner of slaves, but a physician and healer who disliked war. S. P. Gaillard saw in his father's treatment as a prisoner of war in 1865 the foreshadowing of "humiliation and tragedy" felt by white Southerners during Reconstruction. His words below, which begin dispassionately but quickly change, remain a vivid testimonial to what his grandfather, Thomas Gaillard, called "this terrible war."

Dr. Samuel Septimus Gaillard ... served throughout the Civil war, entering the service as a First Lieutenant in the 42nd Alabama Regiment; ... was captured in the fall of Vicksburg, was promptly exchanged and later served as surgeon; was again captured at the fall of Fort Blakely on Mobile Bay and was among those prisoners that suffered cruelty and humiliation on Ship Island, near Biloxi, Mississippi, at the hands of colored troops ...

Reconstruction ... enforced by soldiers' bayonets left a bitter taste in my memory. I, S. P. Gaillard, saw it.

FOR FURTHER READING

The American Civil War: A Military History by the British historian John Keegan stands out from all other single-volume accounts. Keegan is especially good at drawing connections between America's total war of 1861 to 1865 and twentieth-century conflicts. Kent Gramm's excellent *Battle: The Nature and Consequences of Civil War Combat* offers a glimpse of the elusive elephant. Readers interested in the Civil War reenactment phenomenon, as well as other forms of remembrance, should start with *Confederates in the Attic*, Tony Horwitz's often hilarious chronicle of his encounters with the Civil-War obsessed, and "Ted Turner et al. at Gettysburg; or, Re-Enactors in the Attic," Philip D. Beidler's scathing assessment of the Hollywood epic *Gettysburg*. And for more about the Mobile campaign and the Battle of Fort Blakely, readers should consult Arthur W. Bergeron's *Confederate Mobile* and the website for Blakeley State Park (http://www.blakeleypark.com/), which contains links to some excellent online articles.

— STEVEN TROUT

INDEX